THE COURT OF
THE EUROPEAN COMMUNITIES:
NEW DIMENSION IN
INTERNATIONAL ADJUDICATION

by

WERNER FELD

Louisiana State University, New Orleans

THE HAGUE / MARTINUS NIJHOFF / 1964

PRINTED IN THE NETHERLANDS

90 247 0349 2

THE COURT OF THE EUROPEAN COMMUNITIES:
NEW DIMENSION IN INTERNATIONAL ADJUDICATION

TABLE OF CONTENTS

Table of contents   v

Preface   VII

INTRODUCTION   I

I. INSTITUTIONAL SETTING   5

II. ORGANIZATION OF THE COURT   14
    The Judges   14
    The Advocates-General   21
    Obligations and Rights   23
    The Registrar of the Court   25
    The Attachés of the Court   26
    The Chambers of the Court   27
    The Backgrounds of the Top Personnel of the Court   29

III. THE JURISDICTION OF THE COURT   34
    Access to the Court   34
    Classification of Jurisdictional Powers   36
  A. The Court as an International Tribunal   37
  B. The Court as a Constitutional Tribunal   38
    The Powers of the Communities' Organs   40
    Relations Between the Communities and the Member States   45
    Uniform Interpretation of the Treaties   54
    Revision of Treaties   60
    Miscellaneous Functions of a Constitutional Nature   63
  C. The Court as an Administrative Tribunal   65
    Appeals by Private Parties   66
    Notable Litigations   71

Table of contents

D. The Civil Jurisdiction of the Court   80
    Civil Service Matters   81
    Liability of the Communities   83
E. Miscellaneous Competences of the Court   85

IV. SOURCES OF LAW   87

V. PROCEDURE   94
    The Written and Oral Phases of the Proceedings   94
    The Language Problem   97
    The Judgment   98
    Review of Judgments   101
    Enforcement of Judgments   104

VI. CONCLUSIONS   106
    The Court's Impact on the Formulation of Public
      Policy   108
    The Court's Contribution to Political Integration   115

    Selected Bibliography   123

    Index   126

PREFACE

If the United States of Europe should become a reality in the future, it is highly probable that the Court of Justice of the European Communities, now sitting in Luxembourg, will be transformed into the supreme court of the new federation. Legal concepts and judicial traditions formed by the judges in Luxembourg will then become a prominent part of the historical background of this new court. However, even now, during the process of economic intergration in Western Europe, the Court of the European Communities has been assuming an increasingly important role in the settlement of conflicts between economic and sometimes political interests. Moreover, through its more than hundred decisions, the Court has been developing a body of "European" case law which, in time, is likely to have favorable implications for the eventual political unification of Europe.

This book is primarily intended as an introduction to the structure and functions of the Court of the European Communities. In this endeavor consideration has also been given to the forces and factors that might affect the judicial decisions of the Court and to the impact which such decisions might have upon economic enterprises and public policy in the Member states of the European Community, better known as the European Common Market. Thus the book should be of value not only to established jurists and interested laymen, but it may also be used as a supplementary text for courses in law and political science, especially those dealing with comparative government and international organization.

My interest in the Court of the European Communities was inspired by Professor Henry L. Mason of Tulane University to whom I would like to express my sincere gratitude for his sound counsel given to me on so many occasions. I would also wish to thank Mr. H. Sperl, Librarian for the Court of Justice, and his staff for their support of my research and their untiring and prompt replies to my many requests for information. I am equally indebted to the staff of the Law Library of the University of Minnesota for their ready response to all my pleas for assistance. Further, I would like to voice my deep appreciation to the editors of the Villanova Law Review for conveying to me all rights regarding the use of an article of mine published in the Fall 1963 issue of that Review. Last, but certainly not least, I would like to thank my devoted and patient wife for valuable editorial assistance and faithful proof reading far "beyond the call of duty."

All translations from French and German into English are my own. For any errors and misinterpretations in these translations as well as in general, I take exclusive responsibility.

Moorhead, Minnesota   W. F.
March 1964

INTRODUCTION

In 1922, the Austrian Count Coudenhove-Kalergi made the prophetic observation that Europe had the following alternatives in the future: "either to overcome all national hostilities and consolidate in a federal union, or sooner or later succumb to a Russian conquest." [1] During the last decade, Europe seems to have chosen the first alternative and has taken the first, though halting, steps toward the creation of a European Federation. Of course, a federated Europe is far from being assured today. In fact, the French veto of Great Britain's entry into the Common Market and the difficulty of reconciling conflicting agricultural interests between the Common Market partners have produced psychological effects which have resulted in a virtual halt or even a reversal of the movement toward political integration and have reduced, at least temporarily, the prospects of a European Federation. Yet the Paris Treaty establishing in 1952 the European Coal and Steel Community (ECSC), and the Rome Treaties creating in 1958 the European Economic Community (EEC, better known as the Common Market) and the European Atomic Energy Community (Euratom) must be considered as constituting significant steps in the direction of a European Federation. These treaties, signed by France, West Germany, Italy, Belgium, the Netherlands, and Luxembourg, have set up a number of institutions that possess so-called supranational powers. This term signifies that the governments of the signatory states have transferred to these institutions certain limited decision-making powers normally exercised only by the governmental organs of a sover-

---

[1] Quoted by E. N. van Kleffens, "The Case for European Integration; Political Considerations" in C. Grove Haines, *European Integration* (Baltimore, 1957), p. 86.

eign state, powers which include the capability of issuing, under certain specified conditions, binding norms to the inhabitants of the six States.[1] While so far the transfer of such powers has been limited in scope and confined largely to the economic area, a future extension of decision-making authority to other important functional areas of government may imply the emergence of truly "federal" powers and the beginnings of a "federal government" for the six Member States.[2]

The judicial organ provided for in the three Treaties is the Court of Justice of the European Communities. It is the direct successor of the Court of Justice of the European Coal and Steel Community which had been in operation since December 1952. When the European Economic and Atomic Energy Communities were established in 1958, the Coal and Steel Community Court was transformed into the judicial organ for all three Communities. This transformation did not entail any major organizational changes. The "new" court took over from its predecessor the majority of the judges, most of its personnel, its physical plant, and its docket of nearly 40 cases.[3] Located in Luxembourg, the Court occupies at present an unprepossessing, modern office building, devoid of any of the ornate architecture which normally characterizes the home of a high tribunal.

M. Louis Delvaux, one of the Court's justices, has pointed out

---

[1] Cf. also the definition of supranationality by Robert Schuman, one of the 'fathers" of the Coal and Steel Community, in his preface to Paul Reuter's book, *La Communauté Européenne du Charbon et de l'Acier* (Paris, 1953), p. 7; Henry L. Mason, *The European Coal and Steel Community, Experiment in Supranationalism* (The Hague, 1955), p. vii; and Joseph L. Kuns, "Supra-National Organs," *American Journal of International Law* (1952), pp. 690–698.

[2] The term "supranational" has been used in the Treaties underlying the Communities only twice; both times in article 9 of the ECSC Treaty. In addition, it was twice used in the original version of the ECSC Personnel Statute of 1956 (articles 1 and 10). The term was dropped when the Statute was amended in 1961 and it has not been used in the EEC and Euratom Treaties. The reason for this change may be that the term lacks legal clarity and has political rather than legal significance. From the political point of view the term is quite useful because it focuses attention on certain politically important aspects of the Communities. Cf. Ernst B. Haas, *The Uniting of Europe* (Stanford, Cal., 1958), p. 9 and Walter Hallstein, *United Europe, Challenge and Opportunity* (Cambridge, Mass., 1962), pp. 19, 20.

[3] *Journal Officiel des Communautés Européennes* (hereinafter cited as *Journal Officiel*), October 19, 1958, p. 453/58 and November 11, 1958, pp. 467/58 and 468/58.

with justification that the Court possesses in certain respects a "supranational character."[1] While a full explanation of this statement must be deferred to later pages, it can be stated here that the Court's jurisdictional powers far exceed those usually enjoyed by international tribunals of the traditional order and that its judgments against private parties are fully enforceable in the Member States. The breadth of jurisdictional authority has been at least partially responsible for the fact that over the years the Court has assumed a much more important role than was anticipated at its inception.[2] Through many of its over 100 decisions rendered by the end of 1963, it has played an important part in the economic integration process envisioned by the ECSC and EEC Treaties for the Member States. Since it is often difficult to separate economic from political considerations, it is not surprising that some of the Court's decisions have also had certain political implications for the relationships between the Community organs and the Member States and, to a lesser degree, between the Member States themselves.

The basic purpose of this brief volume is to acquaint the un-initiated reader – and there are many on both sides of the Atlantic, including a number of lawyers – with the rather novel institution of adjudication represented by the Court of the European Communities. No claim is made that this is a legal treatise in the narrow sense, but since this volume is concerned with an account of a court, a discussion of relevant legal problems is of course a necessity. However, these problems are not analyzed and evaluated in depth; rather, emphasis is placed on the economic and political implications which some of these problems have within the context of the struggle for a new Europe. It is for this reason, as well as to insure a full understanding of the Court's role, that the first chapter of this volume reviews in some length the institutional framework of the Communities and the position

---

[1] Louis Delvaux, *La Cour de Justice de la Communauté Européenne du Charbon et de l'Acier* (Gembloux, France, 1956), pp. 11, 12.

[2] Cf. Maurice Lagrange, "The Role of the Court of Justice of the European Communities as Seen Through its Case Law," *Law and Contemporary Problems* (Summer, 1961), pp. 400–417 at p. 416.

3

of the Court within this framework. This is followed by an examination of the organization of the Court, the scope of its jurisdictional authority, the sources of law it has used in its decisions, and the procedural methods and techniques employed by the Court. In the final chapter, tentative conclusions are drawn regarding the impact of the Court's decisions upon the formulation of policy by the organs of the Communities and by the governments of the Member States and with respect to the significance which the Court and its case law may have for the political integration of Western Europe.

CHAPTER I

INSTITUTIONAL SETTING

The Court of Justice is one of the two major institutions which are common to the otherwise separate three European Communities. The other common institution is the European Parliament. Its 142 delegates at present are appointed by the members of the legislatures of the Member States, but the Treaties make provisions for their eventual election by direct, universal suffrage and proposals to implement these provisions have already been made by the Parliament.[1] The Parliament has 36 members each from France, West Germany, and Italy, 14 each from Belgium and the Netherlands, and six from Luxembourg. The parliamentary delegations reflect the political composition of the six national legislatures. Three major party groupings exist, namely, the Christian Democrats, the Socialists, and the Liberals and affiliates. In every debate, these groups decide their lines of action, and the members of the European Parliament usually vote along party rather than national lines.[2]

The Communist parties are not represented in the European Parliament. In those national legislatures where their delegations are relatively strong such as in Italy and France, they have been excluded by majority vote of the other parties. In other legislatures Communist parties were either non-existent such as in Germany where the Communist party is banned, or they were so small that mathematically they did not qualify for even one deputy to the European Parliament.

---

[1] Article 21 ECSC Treaty as amended, article 138 EEC Treaty, and article 108 Euratom Treaty. See also Parlement Européen, *Rapport sur les compétences et les pouvoirs du Parlement Européen*, Document No. 31 (June 14, 1963), p. 25.
[2] Cf. Haas, *op.cit.*, pp. 390–450.

The executive functions of the Communities are carried out by four separate bodies, namely, the High Authority of the ECSC, the Commissions of the EEC and Euratom, and the Council of Ministers. Formally the Treaties provide for three Councils of Ministers; in practice, however, the three Communities "share" one Council.[1] Nevertheless, it must be understood that the functions and powers of the Council in specific situations depend on the Treaty under which it is operating.

There is a distinct difference in the composition and character of the High Authority and the Commissions on one side, and the Council of Ministers on the other. The High Authority and the EEC Commission each consists of nine members of whom no more than two can be of the same nationality. The Euratom Commission is composed of five members all of whom must be of a different nationality. The members of these three organs are appointed for a period of several years by the governments of the Member States, acting in common agreement. Once appointed, however, they become independent of the Member States and represent only the interests of the Communities. The decisions of the three bodies are taken by simple majority.[2]

The Council is composed of one Minister from each of the Member governments. Depending on the subject matter to be discussed at a specific meeting of the Council, the attending Minister may be the Foreign Minister, the Minister of Economics, the Minister of Agriculture or any other Minister who might be concerned with the matter under consideration. The Council is the organ in which the national interests of the Member States

[1] Hallstein, *op.cit.*, p. 25.
[2] Cf. articles 9–13 ECSC Treaty, 155–163 EEC Treaty, and 124–132 Euratom Treaty. The appointment procedure under the ECSC Treaty is somewhat more complicated than under the other two treaties. The ninth member of the High Authority is elected by the other eight appointed members.

There have been complaints that in recent years the members of the High Authoriy have not been as independent of the governments of the Member States as the Treaty requires. Allegedly, there has been considerable consultation between the High Authority and these governments in matters which were entirely within the competence of the High Authority and some of its members are said to have followed instructions of their governments rather than to have acted completely independently. (See Parlement Européen, *Debats* (1963), Document No. 64, pp. 80, 81.)

are represented, yet it also performs very important functions for the Communities. In general, it corresponds to the central organ found in all international organizations, but its decisions, unlike those taken by the central organ of most international organizations, are taken in many instances, and in the case of the EEC increasingly, by weighted majorities instead of by unanimous vote.[1]

The High Authotity of the ECSC and the Commissions of the EEC and Euratom collaborate with the Council of Ministers in governing their respective Communities. In addition to their executive authority, these organs also possess certain individual and joint quasi-legislative powers,[2] but the distribution of powers between the High Authority and the Council is quite different from the power relationship between the Commissions and the Council.

Under the ECSC Treaty, the decision-making power is largely concentrated in the High Authority. In most cases, including the issuance of quasi-legislative regulations, this organ can act either with complete independence or may only be required to consult the Council before taking action. Only in instances in which its acts may effect a substantial part of the national economy of the Member States or where co-operation between the Member States seem to be a necessity, is a concurring vote of the Council a requirement for action by the High Authority.[3] In only a few cases is the Council authorized to act by itself; [4] most of its actions are predicated upon a recommendation of the High Authority which requires concurrence by the Council to become effective as an individual decision or as a quasi-legislative rule.

Under the Rome Treaties the respective roles of the Commissions have been reduced in importance and the most prominent powers have been vested in the Council. In many cases the

[1] Cf. articles 26–30 ECSC Treaty, 145–154 EEC Treaty, and 115–123 Euratom Treaty.
[2] For instance article 50(2) ECSC, article 10(2) EEC Treaty, article 186(1) Euratom Treaty.
[3] For instance article 66(3) ECSC Treaty.
[4] See article 9(2).

Commissions of the EEC and Euratom can only propose, whereas the Council has the authority to make the final decision. Yet two important factors in this relationship must be noted. First, the Council can in most instances act only after it has received a proposal from the Commissions. Second, in the majority of cases, the Council has only the right to adopt the proposals of the Commissions by a qualified majority or to reject them; if it desires to amend the proposals it can only do so by a unanimous vote.[1] As a consequence, unless the Council can achieve unanimity within its body, all it can do is to accept the views of the Commissions or leave unsolved the problem involved in the proposal. Moreover, even if unanimity can be achieved, the Council cannot take a decision unless a proposal has been submitted by one of the Commissions. In this sense the Commissions share to a certain degree in the quasi-legislative and executive powers of the Council; indeed they are the initiators of policy and the driving force behind the Council. In addition, in some instances the Council has delegated to the Commission quasi-legislative powers for the issuance of ordinances pertaining primarily to the regulation of technical problems.[2]

The greater powers of the Council of Ministers under the Rome Treaties reflect the fact that under these Treaties the national interests at stake are much more extensive than under the Coal and Steel Treaty. Therefore it was felt by the drafters of the Treaties that the powers of the Commissions had to be more restricted than those of the High Authority. Moreover, the EEC Treaty, in contrast to the ECSC Treaty, does not lay down a detailed program and only states the ends to be sought. In such a novel and potentially far-reaching undertaking as the creation

---

[1] For instance articles 55, 149 EEC Treaty and article 31 (2) and 119 Euratom Treaty.

[2] See for instance Council regulation No. 20, based on articles 42, 43 EEC Treaty (*Journal Officiel*, April 20, 1962, pp. 945/62–952/62). For more details see Gerhard Bebr, *Judicial Control of the European Communities* (New York, 1962), pp. 14–20, and Paul Reuter, "Juridical and Institutional Aspects of the European Regional Communities," *Law and Contemporary Problems* (Summer, 1961), pp. 381–399, particularly 383–392.

of a general Common Market, the six States were anxious to retain a large measure of control over all future developments.

In practice the cooperation and collaboration between the Council and the Commissions is very close. The Council is constantly bombarded by the EEC Commission with new proposals; if one proposal of the Commission does not find the approval of the Council, it is altered or a new one is substituted. Through this close cooperation and interplay of ideas it has been possible on many occasions to overcome the objections of one or more of the Member States to certain measures that the respective governments had viewed as possibly harmful to certain sectors of their national economies.

The Parliament is not authorized to legislate nor does it have full budgetary control. Yet it does have certain powers over the High Authority, the Commissions, and the Council which enable it to influence the quasi-legislative and executive powers of these organs. The three bodies must submit to the Parliament annual reports including their proposed budgets which become the basis for parliamentary debates. In addition, the members of the three organs must answer questions put to them in hearings conducted by parliamentary committees and the reports produced by these committees have proven to be valuable and often influential. Finally, the Parliament may compel the members of the High Authority and the two Commissions to resign *en bloc* by passing a vote of "no confidence" with a two-thirds majority.[1] While a motion for such a vote with regard to the High Authority can only be introduced once a year when the Parliament discusses the annual report of that organ, the introduction of a motion of censure concerning the activities of the Commissions is possible at any time. This power has not been used so far, but it constitutes a threat which can be applied to make the Parliament's will felt in the deliberations and decisions of these organs. Although it is much too early to speak of a parliamentary control over the High Authority and the Commissions because the Parliament at present

[1] Article 23, 24 ECSC Treaty, 140, 144 EEC Treaty, and 110, 114, Euratom Treaty.

lacks real legislative and budgetary powers, nevertheless the relationship between these institutions foreshadows the possibility of a future European parliamentary regime.[1]

The association between the Council and the Parliament is quite different. A collegiate responsibility of the Council to the Parliament does not exist, but on most major decisions of policy the latter institution has a right to be consulted by the Council of Ministers. In particular under the EEC and Euratom Treaties, the Council must seek the opinion of the Parliament in certain instances when it desires to take action upon a proposal submitted by either of the Commissions.[2] Although the Council is not bound by the Parliament's opinion, this procedure provides an opportunity to influence the Council's decision; parliamentary views have on several occasions led to modifications of proposals put before the Council and therefore of the measures finally decided upon.[3] The different character of the relationship between Council and Parliament is also reflected by the fact that the Council has the right to call the Parliament into special session and that the Council's members must be heard by Parliament upon their request. Parliament does not have a reciprocal right with regard to Council members, although in practice the latter have found it politically expedient to appear before the Parliament when so requested.[4]

It is obvious from this brief survey that the Treaties have relegated the Parliament to a secondary role in the direct exercise of the Communities' powers.[5] The Parliament has not been given the legal tools to wield full political control over the executive organs

---

[1] Reuter, *op.cit.*, p. 383.

[2] For instance article 14, (7) EEC Treaty.

[3] Hallstein, *op.cit.*, p. 25.

[4] Gerhard Bebr, "The Balance of Powers in the European Communities," *European Yearbook*, Vol. 5 (1959), pp. 53–79, p. 64.

[5] Brief mention must be made here of the Economic and Social Committee, a joint institution of the EEC and Euratom, and of the Consultative Committee of the Coal and Steel Community. These Committees are composed mainly of representatives of producers, workers, professions and consumers. The Economic and Social Committee consists of 101 members, the Consultative Committee of between 30 and 51. The functions of these committees are purely consultative; although they must be consulted in certain instances, there is no obligation on the part of the executive organs of the Communities to follow their advice. Nevertheless, the two committees,

of the Communities. Moreover, while the executive organs have been endowed with quasi-legislative powers, the Parliament has no authority to legislate. Yet, over the years, the Parliament has been able to steadily increase its political influence over the policies of the Communities. This has been accomplished through intense discussions of the developments in the Communities on the floor of Parliament as well as through excellent parliamentary reports and persistent inquiries about every possible aspect of the executive organs' activities. In addition, at times, the parliamentary groupings have used their counterparts in the national legislatures to bring pressure to bear on the national governments and through them on the Ministers sitting on the Council.[1]

There may be some question as to whether the trend toward greater political power of the Parliament is continuing at present. During the debate of the annual report of the High Authority in June of 1963, an event which should have been of major importance because several, rather serious attacks had been levelled against the activities of that organ, the vast majority of the seats in the Parliament was empty and the discussion was quite brief. While some of the absenteeism could have been explained by the government crises in Italy and the Netherlands which required the presence of many deputies, it must be kept in mind that the entire delegations from these countries account only for one third of the members of the European Parliament. Therefore it seems to be more likely that the extensive absenteeism and the briefness of the debate were symptomatic of a reduced enthusiasm among the members of the Parliament to carry on their drive for stronger power of their institution. The frustration and discouragement experienced by many members of Parliament because of de Gaulle's European policies have undoubtedly been a major factor in this deflation of their enthusiasm.[2]

sounding boards for various interest groups, have gained a certain measure of political influence. For more details see articles 18 and 19 ECSC Treaty, 193–198 EEC Treaty, and 165–170 of the Euratom Treaty. Cf. also Gerda Zellentin, "The Economic and Social Committee," *Journal of Common Market Studies* (1962), pp. 22–28.

[1] Cf. Bebr, "Balance of Powers," pp. 63–67 and 72–75.
[2] The writer attended this particular session of the Parliament.

Regardless of the degree of political influence which the Parliament might have gained over the years, it cannot be considered as sufficient to constitute effective political control over the extensive authority of the Council, the High Authority, and the Commissions. Yet this authority is not unchecked. The Treaties have provided for a far-reaching judicial control of the organs endowed with the executive and quasi-legislative powers of the Communities. This control is exercised by the Court of Justice which has the task "to ensure observance of law and justice in the interpretation and application" of the Treaties.[1] In order to discharge this responsibility, the Court has been given comprehensive jurisdiction over the other organs of the Communities which will be treated in detail later.[2] Suffice it to state here that the Court plays an important role in the maintenance of a balanced distribution of powers among the institutions of the Communities, and that it is itself an important part in the equilibrium of power which the Treaties have established.

From this statement it must not be inferred, however, that the jurisdictional powers of the Court are the same under all three Treaties. Rather, these powers differ; in certain areas the Court's jurisdiction is wider under the ECSC Treaty while in other areas it is more extensive under the EEC and Euratom Treaties. For instance, private enterprises can file actions against the High Authority more liberally than against the Commissions.[3] On the other hand, under the EEC and Euratom Treaties private parties can appeal not only acts of the Commissions, but of the Council as well, which is not possible under the ECSC Treaty.[4]

It would be erroneous to assume that the Court's judicial control over executive organs of the Communities is more or less synonymous with political control or that the Court has taken

[1] Articles 164 EEC Treaty and 136 Euratom Treaty; similar, article 31 ECSC Treaty.

[2] See pp. 34–86 *infra*.

[3] Compare articles 33(2) ECSC Treaty with 173(2) of the EEC Treaty and see the Court's judgment in the case of Groupement des Industries Sidérurgiques Luxembourgeoises v. High Authority, Dec. Nos. 7/54 and 9/54, April 23, 1956, 2 *Recueil de la Jurisprudence de la Cour* (hereinafter referred to as Rec.) 53, (1956) p. 87.

[4] Articles 173 (1) and (2) EEC Treaty and article 146 (1) and (2) Euratom Treaty.

over that part of the political control which the Parliament cannot exercise. Conceptually, judicial and political control are quite different. Political control by the Parliament involves the formulation of independent value judgments regarding the activities of the executives through majority or unanimous votes by the members of the Parliament. Judicial control of the activities of the executives, on the other hand, involves the application of rules formulated by a "legislative body," namely, the framers of the Treaties in cooperation with the legislatures of the Member States which had to ratify the Treaties. While in the application of these rules the judges may have an opportunity to reflect their own political values and beliefs and may even be in a position to make new law, they are nevertheless bound in general by the value judgments expressed by the framers of the Treaties. In addition, judicial control also extends to the Parliament; at least under the ECSC Treaty, the Court may annul a resolution of the Parliament "on the grounds of lack of competence or major violations of procedure." [1] Another conceptual difference between political and judicial control lies in the fact that the former primarily influences the policy formulation of the Communities' organs and provides only general supervision over the exercise of their powers, whereas the latter affords an immediate and specific remedy against particular acts of the organs of the Communities.

[1] Article 38. Cf. also Hans-Joachim Seeler, "Politische Integration and Gewaltenteilung," *Europa-Archiv* (1960), pp. 13–24, and K. H. Mattern, "Rechtsgrundlage and Praxis der Montanversammlung," *Neue Juristische Wochenschrift* (1954), pp. 218–219 at p. 219.

13

CHAPTER II

ORGANIZATION OF THE COURT

The Judges

The Court is composed of seven judges who are appointed with the "common consent" of the governments of the Member States. The Treaties do not specify the nationality of the judges. However, the personnel statutes of the Communities require all civil servants – and the judges are civil servants in a broad sense – to be nationals of the Member States, although exceptions to this rule can be made.[1] So far, only nationals of the six Membeı States have occupied seats on the bench.

Normally, the judges are appointed for a term of six years. However, in order to stagger their terms of office, three of the first seven appointees, who were chosen by lot, held office only for three years, and thereafter three or four judges respectively were appointed every three years. The judges may be re-appointed after the expiration of their terms, and their total number may be increased by the Council of Ministers acting unanimously upon the request of the Court.[2]

The judges must be chosen from among persons of "indisputable independence" who are qualified to hold the highest judicial office in their respective countries or who are jurists of high standing.[3] These qualifications are stricter than those contained originally in the ECSC Treaty which did not require the prospective judges to be jurists, but merely persons of "recognized

[1] Article 28(a). (For the text of the EEC and Euratom personnel statutes see *Journal Officiel*, June 14, 1962; the ECSC personnel statutes, promulgated earlier but later amended, are virtually identical.)
[2] Articles 32, 32b ECSC Treaty, 165, 167 EEC Treaty and 137, 139 Euratom Treaty.
[3] Articles 32b ECSC Treaty, 167 EEC Treaty, and 139 Euratom Treaty.

independence and competence." [1] The justices of the Court may be removed from office only if, in the unanimous opinion of the other members of the Court, they no longer fulfill the required conditions or meet the obligations of their office. They may, of course, submit their voluntary resignation from the Court at any time, and since the inception of the Court a few of the judges have vacated their offices in this manner. [2]

The judges elect from among their members the president of the Court for a term of three years and this term is renewable. However, the first president of the Coal and Steel Community Court was not to be elected but was appointed by the Member governments and the same procedure was prescribed and used for the selection of the first president of the Court of the three Communities. [3]

Besides directing the work of the Court and presiding over its sessions and deliberations, the president possesses other important powers. He may suspend the forced execution of a judgment of the Court or of a decision of the Communities' executive organs imposing pecuniary obligations on private persons. He may grant a stay in the execution of an action against which an appeal has been lodged with the Court, and he may issue interim orders. However, such rulings of the president are provisional and in no way prejudge the decisions of the Court on the substance of the matter before it. [4] Outside the realm of the Court, the president performs a very influential function by presiding over the "Committee of the Presidents" of the Coal and Steel Community. This committee is composed of the presidents of the Court, the

---

[1] Article 32 prior to amendment at the time the EEC and Euratom Treaties came into force.

[2] Articles 32b, ECSC Treaty, 167 EEC Treaty, 139 Euratom Treaty and 5 and 6 of the Protocol on the Statute of the Court of Justice (EEC Treaty). The Protocols of the other Treaties on the Statute have similar provisions.

[3] Articles 32b(5) ECSC Treaty, 167(5) EEC Treaty, and 139(5) Euratom Treaty in connection with Section 5(1) of the Convention containing the Transitional Provisions (ECSC Treaty) and articles 11, 10 ECSC Treaty, 244(1) EEC Treaty, and 212(1) Euratom Treaty.

[4] Article 36 of the Statute (EEC Treaty) with articles 185, 186, 187, 192 of the EEC Treaty. Similar provisions are found in the other Treaties. See also article 6 of the Rules of Procedure.

High Authority, the Parliament, and the Council. It plays a very prominent role in the fiscal and personnel administration of that Community.[1]

Thirteen judges have been members of the Court since its inception in 1952; two of them, Mr. Louis Delvaux of Belgium and Mr. Ch. Leon Hammes of Luxembourg have served the Court continuously until the present. Three of the justices of the original Court, Mr. Massimo Pilotti of Italy, the first president, Mr. Joseph Serrarens and Mr. Adrianus van Kleffens, both from the Netherlands, served until 1958. When the Court of the European Communities came into being, they were replaced by Mr. A. M. Donner, a Dutchman, who became president of the Court, and by Mr. Rino Rossi and Mr. Nicola Catalano, both of Italy. The latter was succeeded in March of 1962 by Mr. Alberto Trabucchi, also of Italy, and two months later, Mr. Jacques Rueff of France, a member of the original Court, was replaced by Mr. Robert Lecourt, his compatriot. Finally, Mr. Otto Riese, the German member of the original Court, was succeeded in April 1963 by his fellow countryman, Mr. Walter Strauss. Thus today the Court is composed of the following justices: Donner, Delvaux, Hammes, Rossi, Trabucchi, Lecourt, and Strauss.[2]

The provisions of the Treaties concerning the terms of office of the judges and the methods of their appointment have been subjected to criticism. It has been claimed that a term of office lasting six years was too short and that as a minimum the Statute of the International Court of Justice should have been emulated which stipulates a term of nine years for the judges of that court.[3] Further, it has been asserted that a six year term, coupled with the possibility of re-appointment, might tend to operate against the independence of the judge since for a re-appointment the judge must by necessity look to his government.[4] Although the

---

[1] Article 78 (3) ECSC Treaty.

[2] Hammes, Rueff, and Serrarens are the judges of the original Court who were chosen by lot to serve only three years in their first terms. Delvaux, Hammes, and Catalano were the first "three-year" judges of the present Court.

[3] Article 13 of the Statute of the International Court of Justice.

[4] Mason, *op.cit.*, p. 25, who relates the thoughts of the French Economic Council

appointment of a judge requires the "common consent" of the six governments which implies the possibility of a veto, in practice the consent is a formality. A pattern has developed according to which the positions of judges and other important court personnel are assigned to different countries and which appears to allot special weight to the office of the president. This is reflected by the fact that when Mr. Pilotti was president of the Court, Italy had only one judge and the Netherlands had two. However, when Mr. Donner became the president, the ratio between the two countries was reversed. While France, Germany, and Belgium have been allotted only one judgeship, they are compensated by the allocation of one advocate-general [1] each to France and Germany and by the assignment of the post of registrar to Belgium. Luxembourg, as the smallest country, has been allotted only one judgeship. Of course, even within this pattern, the government of one Member State could veto a particular nomination of another government. However, the fear of retaliation against future nominations excludes in practice the use of such a veto.[2]

An informal agreement among the six governments as to the distribution of the posts of presidents between the executive organs and the Court also has a bearing on the pattern of positions within the Court. At the present time, the presidency of the EEC Commission is held by a German, the presidency of the Euratom Commission by a Frenchman, the chief executive of the High Authority is an Italian, and the president of the Court a national of the Netherlands. When after the expiration of Mr. Donner's first term as president the suggestion was made to nominate Mr. Riese, the German judge, as a candidate for this post, some of the governments of the Member States objected even though according to the Treaties the president is "elected" by the judges of the Court and Mr. Riese might have had the necessary votes

in 1951, and Hans-Ulrich Bächle, *Die Rechtsstellung der Richter am Gerichtshof der Europäischen Gemeinschaften* (Berlin, 1961), pp. 126–130, who also cites other critics.
[1] Their functions are described in detail on pp. 21–23 *infra*.
[2] Bächle, *op.cit.*, p. 62.

for his election. However, the election of Mr. Riese as the Court's president would have obviously disturbed the agreed patterns within the Court and among the major organs of the Communities and thus, for political reasons, the choice of nominees for the presidency of the Court was extremely restricted.[1]

From the foregoing it becomes quite clear that the governments of the Member States have, in practice, the exclusive power of appointing their nationals to the positions on the Court allotted to them. This system differs radically from the method used for the selection of the judges of the International Court of Justice; the judges of that court are elected by the United Nations General Assembly and the Security Council from a list of candidates who are nominated not by their governments but by "national groups." [2]

Since the "governments" appoint the judges, the basic decision for the selection of a prospective justice is made by the cabinet in power in the Member State which has to fill an actual or future vacancy on the Court. In contrast to the practice in the Member States, no participation by the parliament, or any other governmental or political unit, or the highest courts is required. The procedures to be utilized for the selection of an individual to serve as a judge of the Court are entirely within the discretion of the government.[3] In essence, then, the selection of a judge is a politi-

---

[1] Cf. *Nieuwe Rotterdamse Courant*, October 12, 1961.

[2] Article 4 of the Statute of the International Court of Justice. For details regarding the complicated process of nomination see Shabtai Rosenne, *The International Court of Justice* (Leyden, 1961), pp. 122–125.

[3] Newspaper reports and conversations of the writer with officials of the Ministry of Justice in Bonn revealed the following procedures for the appointment of a judge of the Court at the present time. Suggestions of candidates are normally made by the Ministries of Justice, Economics, and Scientific Research. A provisional decision is then made by the Cabinet which is transmitted to the Court for informal approval and after that to the governments of the other Member States for their consent. At that time, the parliamentary groupings of *all* parties are also informed, but it is not claer what would be done in case of any objections from any of the parties. Finally, the official Federal Guild of Lawyers (*Bundesrechtsanwaltkammer*) and the Association of Judges and State Prosecutors is advised. In the case of the Strauss appointment, informal sounding out of potential candidates was under way at the Ministry of Justice and possibly the Ministry of Economics since the former Federal Finance Minister Starke seemed to be interested in the judgeship. As soon as the decision was made by the Cabinet to appoint Dr. Strauss, all other efforts ceased and no other

cal decision, although considerations regarding the professional qualifications of the candidate for judgeship necessarily play a very large or possibly even a predominant role. The fact that the appointing government is guided by political motives and will attempt to select a candidate from its own party ranks, is in itself, of course, neither unusual nor contemptible, provided the candidate is fully qualified.[1] Nevertheless, the danger exists that the criterion of party affiliation might be more important for an appointment than professional qualifications or that a not fully qualified individual will be appointed who for domestic political reasons is to be removed from his position within the governmental structure of his country but who for public relations reasons must be given a new position which appears as a promotion.[2]

Since for re-appointment the judges of the Court are exclusively dependent upon their own governments, which are often parties to disputes before the Court, it is certainly within the realm of possibility that they may be tempted on occasion to let thoughts

---

formal nominations were made. Apparently the political parties agreed and no adverse criticism was voiced in the news media although Strauss, formerly Secretary of State in the Justice Department, had been implicated in the Spiegel affair of October 1962 because he failed to inform his superior, Minister Stammberger, of the proceedings planned against the editors of that magazine. (*Frankfurter Allgemeine Zeitung*, December 20, 1962, *Frankfurter Rundschau*, January 15, 1963, and *Deutsche Zeitung*, October 13, 1962, and February 2, 1963.)

In France, the Foreign Minister has currently the primary responsibility for the selection of a justice of the Court but he must consult the Minister of Justice. The final decision rests with the Cabinet. The political parties are neither consulted nor informed, nor is there any discussion regarding the proposed candidate with any professional association. Primarily considered for appointment are professors of public or economic law and justices of the highest courts in France, but other eminent personalities with a legal background are also eligible. (Information obtained from the Legal Service of the French Ministry of Foreign Affairs.)

[1] Mr. Catalano's resignation and Mr. Trabucchi's appointment in 1962 are said to have been strongly motivated by political considerations. Mr. Trabucchi's brother was then Minister of Justice in Rome and Mr. Catalano's re-appointment in the fall of 1961 is supposed to have been made with the understanding that he would resign within a few months in order to make Mr. Trabucchi's appointment possible (*Nieuwe Rotterdamse Courant*, October 12, 1961 and *France Industrielle*, December 26, 1961).

[2] Cf. Bächle, *op.cit.*, pp. 61, 62 and Konrad Zweigert, *Empfiehlt es sich, Bestimmungen über den Rechtsschutz zu ändern?* Paper presented at the Cologne Conference "Ten Years of Jurisprudence of the Court of Justice of the European Communities," April 24–26, 1963.

of the future color their thoughts of the present. If a judge should be denied re-appointment by his government, he might be without employment for some time or be may have to accept a much less desirable position than the one from which he resigned in order to enter the service of the Communities. Mr. Etienne Hirsch's failure to be re-appointed by the French government to the presidency of the Euratom Commission after his first term expired in January of 1962,[1] and the fact that some of the judges of the Coal and Steel Community Court were replaced when it became the Court of the three Communities,[2] undoubtedly will be remembered by the justices of the Court.

Judge Riese has declared in 1958 that the fears that the short term of office and the appointment procedure for the judges would endanger their independence, have proved to be unfounded. He stated that "in no case have the judges been guided by extraneous, political or nationalistic viewpoints." [3] In all likelihood, the statement applies just as much to the present judges as it did when Mr. Riese wrote these words. Yet from an institutional point of view the danger to the independence of the Court's judges continues to exist until the provisions of the Treaties with regard to the length of their terms of office and the methods of their appointments have been changed in such a manner as to fully insure their independence.

A number of valid proposals to attain this objective have been made. With regard to the term of office, it has been suggested that

[1] See *Discours de M. Etienne Hirsch, Président de la Commission devant l'Assemblée Européenne à Strasbourg*, published by the Euratom Commission, December 1961.

[2] Otto Riese, "Erfahrungen aus der Praxis des Gerichtshofes der Europäischen Gemeinschaft für Kohle und Stahl," *Deutsche Richterzeitung* (1958), pp. 270–274, at p. 271. It should be noted that Mr. Pilotti was then in his seventies, but that he as well as Mr. Serrarens and Mr. van Kleffens seemed to have been willing to continue in their jobs. Mr. Serrarens was one of the first "three-year" judges and had only served half of his second full term by the time the Coal and Steel Community Court was transformed into the present tribunal.

[3] Riese, *op.cit.*, p. 271. Similar thoughts were expressed by Mr. Rueff in his farewell statement on May 18, 1962 (Mimeographed copy). In the same vein Hans-Wolfram Daig, "Die vier ersten Urteile des Gerichtshofes der Europäischen Gemeinschaft für Kohle und Stahl," *Juristenzeitung* (1955), pp. 361–373, at p. 371. A different point of view is held by Judge Hammes. See Ch. L. Hammes in *Congresso Internazionale dei Magistrati*, Roma, October 11–13, 1958, Vol. II, pp. 821, 822.

judges should be appointed either for life or at least for twelve years with payment of their full salaries for life. With regard to the method of appointment, it has been proposed to establish a selection committee within the European Parliament or to have the Parliament elect the judges from a list submitted by the governments of the Member States. Another proposal advocates the selection of new judges for position vacancies by the Court itself, possibly from a list prepared by the highest courts in the Member States. In this manner the highest quality of the judges would be assured since normally members of the highest courts are in the best position to evaluate the qualifications of candidates for judgeship. The least desirable proposal appears to be the the adoption of the system used by the International Court of Justice at The Hague since it is extremely complicated and cumbersome.[1] To put into effect any of the above proposals requires a revision of the Treaties. However, the political relations existing at present between the Member States make any revision of the Treaties in the near future a very unlikely undertaking since it is doubtful that agreement by all Member governments for the solution of controversial problems could be obtained.

The Advocates-General

The judges of the Court are assisted by two advocates-general who must meet the same professional qualifications as the judges and who are also appointed for six years by the governments of the Member States. As in the case of the judges, the terms of the two advocates-general are staggered and appointments for one or the other of the two positions are made every three years. Re-appointment is possible and the two advocates-general appointed when the Court of the Coal and Steel Community was established in 1952 are still performing their services at the present time. They are Mr. Maurice Lagrange of France and Mr. Karl Joseph Roemer of Germany. Their functions are "to present publicly, with complete impartiality and independence, reasoned

---

[1] For fuller information see Bächle, *op.cit.*, pp. 57–62 and 126–130 who cites other proposals and Zweigert, *op.cit.*

conclusions on cases submitted to the Court of Justice with a view of assisting the latter in the performance of its duties. . . . "[1]

The advocates-general represent in no way either the Communities or the public; they function only in the interest of justice. Their sole, but vital task is to prepare for the Court an opinion on the legal aspects of any question submitted to it. To carry out this task, they frequently engage in thorough comparative law studies and in a discussion and evaluation of the views of various commentators presented in legal literature. The opinion of the advocate-general is not part of the judgment itself; nor is it necessarily accepted by the Court. However, there is no doubt that the opinions of the advocates-general strongly influence the Court, and their "conclusions" are always published next to the judgment in the collection of the jurisprudence of the Court. It is significant that in the more than one hundred judgments rendered by the Court by the end of 1963, the opinions of the advocates-general have been accepted by the justices in the majority of the cases. If they are not accepted, they take on the character of dissenting opinions and as such frequently offer alternative solutions which may be of relevance for the development of future case law.

Although the institution of the advocate-general is unknown in Common Law systems, it is extensively used in French administrative law procedure. In fact, the advocate-general in the judicial organization of the Communities is modeled after the Government Commissioner of the French Conseil d'Etat, the most important of the French administrative courts and the apex of the French administrative court system.[2]

The advocates-general may be removed from office under the same conditions as the judges, namely, if they do not meet any longer the requirements of their office or can not carry out the

---

[1] Articles 32a and b ECSC Treaty, 166, 167, EEC Treaty, and 138, 139 Euratom Treaty.

[2] Delvaux, *op.cit.*, p. 14. For additional information see D. G. Valentine, *The Court of Justice of the European Coal and Steel Community* (The Hague, 1955), pp. 44–48, and Bernard Schwartz, *French Administrative Law and the Common Law World* (New York, 1954), pp. 23–41 and 138–9.

obligations imposed on them by their office. While the power of removal is now vested in the Court itself, under the ECSC Treaty the decision had to be made by the Council of Ministers in an unanimous vote after having received appropriate advice from the Court.[1] The number of advocates-general can be increased by the Council voting unanimously if a request to this effect has been made by the Court.[2]

Obligations and Rights

The justices of the Court and the advocates-general have generally the same obligations and immunities. Before entering upon their duties they must swear an oath to perform their duties impartially and conscientiously, and to preserve the secrecy of the Court's deliberations. The oath may be taken in the form prescribed by the national law of the individual justice or advocate-general. Immediately after they are sworn in, they must make a solemn declaration "that, both during and after their term of office, they will respect the obligations resulting therefrom, in particular the duty of exercising honesty and discretion as regards the acceptance, after their term of office, of certain functions and advantages." [3] This declaration was not required under the original Statute of the Court of the Coal and Steel Community and was added when the Court Statutes of the EEC and Euratom Treaties were framed.

The Statutes stipulate that which appears to be quite obvious in the case of a high tribunal, namely, that the judges and advocates-general may not hold any political or administrative office. Nor may they engage in any paid or unpaid professional activities unless a special exemption is granted by the Council of Ministers. Finally, they may not participate in the settlement of any case in which they have previously participated as a repre-

---

[1] Articles 6–8 Statute of the Court (EEC), article 13 of the ECSC Statute of the Court, and article 4 of the Convention Relating to Certain Institutions Common to the European Communities.

[2] Article 32a ECSC Treaty, 166 EEC Treaty, and 138 Euratom Treaty.

[3] Article 4 Statute of the Court (EEC Treaty); see also article 2 of that Statute and Article 3 of the Rules of Procedure of the Court (*Journal Officiel*, January 18, 1960).

sentative, counsel, or advocate of one of the parties, or in which they have been called upon to decide as a member of a tribunal, of a commission of inquiry or in any other capacity. In cases of difficulties in the application of these provisions the Court is called upon to make a decision.[1]

The Treaties endow the judges and advocates-general with certain specific immunities and privileges. First, they are granted immunity from legal process regarding any acts performed by them in their official capacity including anything that they have written or spoken, and this immunity continues after the ending of their term. This immunity, however, may be lifted by the Court sitting in plenary session. In that event a penal action may be brought against a judge or an advocate-general, but such a case is justiciable within any of the Member States only before the tribunal competent to try judges belonging to "the highest national judiciary." [2] The suspension of the immunity from legal process appears to be limited to penal action and is not permitted if civil actions such as breach of contract or defamation are involved.[3]

Second, the judges and advocates-general, as all officials of the Communities, enjoy in each of the Member States exemption from any tax on their salaries. They may also import free of duty their household effects when taking up their position in Luxembourg, and may remove them free of tax to their own country at the end of their term of office. Furthermore, neither they nor their families are to be subject to any immigration restrictions or formalities.[4]

---

[1] Articles 4 and 16 of the Statute (EEC Treaty). The Statute of the International Court of Justice contains similar provisions. Article 4 of the ECSC Statute also forbids the judges and advocates-general "to acquire or hold, directly or indirectly, any interest in any business related to coal or steel during their term of office and during a period of three years thereafter." For additional information, particularly regarding the differences between the ECSC Treaty and the Rome Treaties, see Werner Feld, "The Judges of the Court of Justice of the European Communities," *Villanova Law Review* (Fall 1963), pp. 37–58, especially pp. 48–50.

[2] Article 3 of the Statute of the Court (EEC and Euratom Treaties). The ECSC Statute is similar.

[3] Valentine, *op.cit.*, p. 44.

[4] Articles 11b, c, d, and e, and 12(2) of the Protocol on the Privileges and Immuni-

Third, the judges and advocates-general benefit from a provision in the personnel statutes of the Communities which requires each institution to furnish assistance to their civil servants in case of threats, insults, libel, and other attacks that may be aimed at them or their families because of their official positions or their official activities. The Communities are obliged to compensate the affected civil servant fòr damages suffered unless he can obtain indemnification from the malefactor.[1]

The Registrar of the Court

The registrar of the Court fulfills a very important role. He is not only the chief administrator of the Court, but also assists in the conduct of the Court's judicial business. During the public sessions of the Court, he wears a robe as do the judges and advocates-general. Requests to bring actions before the Court must be addressed to the registrar. He prepares the official record of the evidence of each witness as well as the record of each session of the Court, both of which must be signed by him and the president. Finally, he is required, together with the president, to sign the judgments of the Court.[2]

As chief administrative officer, the registrar is in charge of the personnel of the Court. He is responsible for the proper maintenance of the official register of the Court and for the handling of the archives and publications. He has custody of the seals and supervises the activities of the Court's library. He is also entrusted with the maintenance of the physical plant of the Court.[3]

The registrar is elected by the judges of the Court from among the candidates previously nominated by one or more of the justices. Prior to the election, the advocates-general must be consulted. The candidate receiving a majority of votes is elected,

---

ties of the Community (EEC Treaty). The same provisions are found in the Protocols of the other two Treaties.

[1] Article 24 of the Personnel Statutes.

[2] Articles 19, 30 and 34 of the Statute (EEC Treaty) and articles 47(6), 53 of the Rules of Procedure.

[3] Article 11 of the Statute(EEC Treaty) and article 15–17 of the Rules of Procedure. See also Delvaux, *op.cit.*, p. 17.

and in a similar manner the Court may elect one or several assistant registrars. The term of office of the registrar is six years and he is eligible for re-election. Before taking office, he is required to take the same oath as the judges.[1]

The immunities of the registrar are not as far-reaching as those of the judges and advocates-general. In particular, he can not claim the same wide exemption from legal process, but only enjoys the limited immunity from legal process accorded to all civil servants of the Communities which under certain circumstances can be withdrawn by the president of the Court.[2]

The registrar can only be dismissed if he no longer fulfills the required conditions for holding his office or can not meet the obligations of his office. Relief from office is a decision which the Court must make after allowing the registrar to state his case and after hearing the advocates-general.[3] However, neither the Treaties, nor the Statutes and Rules of Procedure set forth precisely the conditions of the registrar's office which are to be fulfilled. It has been suggested, therefore, that the necessary criteria may be found in the oath of office of the registrar.[4] From this oath it may be implied that the registrar must perform his functions impartially and conscientiously and that he must preserve the secrecy of the Court's deliberations.

The Attachés of the Court

Each judge and advocate-general has an assistant of his own nationality who has legal training and whose major task it is to prepare for his chief pre-trial studies on the legal questions involved in a case before the Court. These assistants are called attachés and are appointed for life. Even when the judges change, the attachés remain and aid the incoming judge of their own

---

[1] Article 11(1) to (5) and article 3(1) of the Rules of Procedure.

[2] Article 11a, 17 and 20 of the Protocol on the Immunities and Privileges of the Community (EEC Treaty). The immunity can be withdrawn if such withdrawal does not contravene the interest of the Communities.

[3] Article 11, (6) of the Rules of Procedure.

[4] Valentine, *op.cit.*, p. 53. For the wording of the oath see article 9 of the Statute (EEC Treaty).

nationality in acquainting himself with the practices and procedures of the Court. Since the studies which they prepare for their chiefs frequently involve a detailed examination of the different laws in the Member States and a thorough research of legal literature, their knowledge of the Community law is outstanding. In addition, their linguistic capabilities are in some instances greater than those of the judges and advocates-general they serve.[1]

Because of their thorough legal knowledge and because of their appointment for life, the attachés, mostly bright, young men, are a significant factor for the continuity of the law developed by the Court. On the other hand, the danger exists that a bureaucracy is growing up which will gradually take over the functions that should be performed by the judges and the advocates-general.[2] For this reason, it might be better to institute a system of law clerks similar to that used by the judges of the United States Supreme Court.[3] Under such a system the attachés would normally serve only a period of one to three years, but in any case not longer than the term of office of the judge or advocate-general to whom they are assigned. Thus, their possible influence on the deliberations and decisions of the justices of the Court and the advocates-general would be materially curtailed, but their general usefulness would be retained.

The Chambers of the Court

In principle, the Court sits in plenary session. However, it is authorized to set up chambers composed of three or five judges and soon after its establishment, the Court created two chambers of three judges each.[4] The functions of these chambers are to undertake preliminary examinations of evidence or to decide

---

[1] Riese, *op.cit.*, p. 271. A number of the most brilliant articles on the law of the Communities have been published by the attachés.

[2] *Ibid.* See also Günther Küchenhoff, "Das System der Sachbearbeiter in der Gerichtsbarkeit," *Die Öffentliche Verwaltung* (1956), pp. 289–292.

[3] Cf. Chester Newland, "Personal Assistants to Supreme Court Justices: The Law Clerks," *Oregon Law Review* (1961), pp. 299–317.

[4] Articles 32 ECSC Treaty, 165 EEC Treaty, 137 Euratom Treaty. See also Valentine, *op.cit.*, p. 40, note 2.

certain categories of cases. The division of tasks between the two chambers is made by the president of the Court.[1]

The presidents of each Chamber are elected by the Court for a period of one year and are eligible for re-election after the expiration of their term. The method of election is the same as that for the president of the Court.[2] The choice of a successor for the post of chamber president is not limited to the judges assigned to a particular chamber.[3]

Certain cases cannot be assigned to the chambers and must be heard by the Court in plenary session. These are cases submitted by a Member State or by one of the institutions of the Communities, or cases referred to the Court for a preliminary decision by a municipal court or tribunal of the Member States.[4] In such cases the Court is required to sit in plenary session for all tasks preparatory to the decision; it cannot direct one of the chambers to hear and examine evidence for the Court as a whole.[5]

At the present time, the First Chamber of the Court is composed of judges Delvaux, Trabucchi, and Strauss, with Mr. Delvaux being its president. Mr. Lagrange is the advocate-general assigned to this chamber. The Second Chamber's president is Mr. Lecourt and he is assisted by judges Hammes and Rossi. The advocate-general of this chamber is Mr. Roemer. Both chambers undertake preliminary examinations of evidence, and both have been assigned to render decisions in certain categories of cases dealing with civil service matters.[6] For all other cases the Court sits in plenary session.

A party to a litigation before the Court can not invoke either the nationality of a judge nor the absence from the bench of a judge of the party's own nationality as grounds to request a change in the composition of the Court or one of its chambers.

---

[1] Article 24 of the Rules of Procedure.
[2] Article 6 of the Rules of Procedure.
[3] Valentine, *op.cit.*, p. 41.
[4] Articles 32 ECSC Treaty, 165 EEC Treaty, and 137 Euratom Treaty.
[5] See E. Wohlfarth, U. Everling, H. J. Glässner, R. Sprung, *Die Europäische Wirtschaftsgemeinschaft, Kommentar zum Vertrag* (Berlin and Frankfurt a.m., 1960), p. 478, comment 3 to article 165.
[6] *Journal Officiel*, October 28, 1961, p. 1257/61 and October 29, 1963, p. 2598/63.

This very commendable new principle which the framers of the Treaties have introduced for the procedure before a multi-national tribunal reflects the supranational character of the Court and tends to bolster the independence of the justices.[1]

The Backgrounds of the Top Personnel of the Court

So far, the organizational structure of the Court has been described and examined. However, in order to gain an insight into the Court as a working institution, one must also have at least a rudimentary knowledge of the education and prior occu-pations of the men who have served and are still serving the Court as judges, advocates-general, and registrar. What are their backgrounds in these respects?

In keeping with the provisions of the ECSC Treaty that the judges of the Court were to be selected from among "persons of recognized independence and competence"[2] and therefore did not need to be jurists, two of the original members of the Court lacked a formal legal education. These gentlemen were Mr. Serrarens and Mr. Rueff. All the other judges had completed their formal law studies, two of them, Mr. Donner and Mr. Trabucchi, receiving their doctor of law degree *cum laude*.

Of the academically trained jurists who have served on the Court, three judges, or less than 30% of the justices, seem to have had substantial previous experience on the bench. They are Justices Hammes, Riese and Rossi. Mr. Pilotti, Mr. van Kleffens and Mr. Strauss also have had judicial experience but their careers as judges appear to have been rather limited. Four of the judges have practiced law or acted as legal counsel to private enterprises or public organizations. They are Catalano, Delvaux, Lecourt and van Kleffens, but none of them seems to have been a practitioner recently. Five of the justices have been professors of law; while for justices Hammes and Catalano the academic careers appeared to have played only a minor role, justices Donner, Riese, and Trabucchi have distinguished themselves as

---

[1] Article 16(4) of the Statute (EEC Treaty), 19(4) ECSC Treaty Statute.
[2] Article 32 ECSC Treaty prior to its amendment. See also pp. 14–15 *supra*.

academicians and have occupied positions of leadership in legal
societies and conferences. Finally, four of the judges, Hammes,
Catalano, Rossi, and Pilotti, performed for short periods of time
the functions of prosecutor in their respective countries.

It is interesting to note that several judges occupied important
executive and administrative positions. Delvaux was for a short
time Belgian Minister of Agriculture in 1946. Lecourt held several
times during the period from 1948 to 1958 the posts of Minister of
Justice; from 1959 to 1961 he was French Minister of State for
Aid and Cooperation between France and Member States of the
French Community, and later for the Overseas Departments and
Territories. Strauss was Secretary of State in the Federal Ministry
of Justice for more than 20 years before being appointed to the
Court of Justice. Riese was also a high official in the German
Ministry of Justice but his service was performed during the late
1920's. Van Kleffens held high positions in the Dutch Ministry of
Economics and Catalano occupied several governmental posts in
Italy. Justice Pilotti was an Italian delegate to several international conferences, and was Assistant Secretary-General of the
League of Nations from 1932 until 1937. Mr. Rueff, "non-jurist,"
had a strong administrative background; he held several very
important posts in the French Ministry of Finance and in 1926
was Minister of Finance in the Cabinet of Mr. Poincaré. He was
sous-gouverneur of the Bank of France in 1939 and was a member
of the French delegation to the United Nations. In addition, he
has been a professor at the *Ecole Libre des Sciences Politiques*.

Several of the judges of the Court have been quite active in
politics. Mr. Delvaux has been a deputy of the Belgian Chamber
of Representatives from 1936 to 1946. Judge Lecourt has been a
member of the French Assembly from 1945 to 1958 and has been
president of the parliamentary group of the Popular Republican
Party (MRP) several times. He was also a member of the executive committee of the European Movement. Finally, Mr.
Serrarens, another "non-jurist," was a member of the Dutch
Senate in 1929, and was a deputy in the Assembly of the Netherlands from 1937 to 1952. In addition, he has participated in many

international labor conferences and has long been active in the international labor movement. He was secretary-general of the International Confederation of Christian Unions from 1920 until 1952. Mr. Strauss participated in the organization of the local Christian Democratic Party in Berlin, but his later efforts to become elected to the *Bundestag* were unsuccessful. He has also been president of the politically influential Protestant Working Group of the Christian Democratic Party.[1]

The variety of backgrounds of the justices of the Court revealed by this brief survey is surprising, especially when one considers that in France, Germany, and may other countries of the Continent of Europe most judges are professionally trained and rise through a career service to the highest judicial positions in their countries. In the United States, a great deal of attention has been focused in recent years upon the question of whether individuals should have had experience on the bench before they are considered eligible for appointment to the Supreme Court. Professor John R. Schmidhauser, in his study of the politics and personalities of the members of the United States Supreme Court comes to the conclusion that "there is little in the history of the Supreme Court to suggest that justices with prior judicial experience were more objective or better qualified than those who lacked such experience." [2] Schmidhauser points out that some of the Court's most distinguished members, among them Marshall, Taney, Hughes, Brandeis, and Stone, were totally lacking in this experience before their appointment to the Supreme Court.

In view of the comprehensive jurisdiction of the Court which entails the solution of legal problems in the economic, social, administrative, and even political sphere, the varied backgrounds and experiences of the judges of the Court may be an advantage.[3]

---

[1] The material on the background of the judges is taken from the *Annuaire-Manuel du Parlement Européen 1961–1962*, pp. 109–112, the *Notice Biographique sur les Membres de la Cour*, October 1954, *Der Spiegel*, January 24, 1962, pp. 24–34, and *Weser-Kurier* (Bremen) November 7, 1962.

[2] John R. Schmidhauser, *The Supreme Court* (New York, 1961), p. 54.

[3] In the ratification proceedings of the ECSC Treaty in the German *Bundestag* one of the deputies stated that "the Court of Justice must not be merely a collection of

Indeed, if the three Communities and their institutions may be viewed as the possible forerunners of a federal governmental system for the Member States, the broad knowledge possessed by some of the justices in the fields of economics, finance, and administration may be a significant factor in arriving at decisions which transcend narrow judicial considerations and which reflect an application of the Treaties with a keen eye on the purpose of the Communities and with an appreciation for the future.[1] The assumption is justified that the diversity of interests, experiences, and values represented in the deliberating sessions of the Court may have stimulated a fertile interchange of concepts and ideas and thus broadened the views of the participants. On the other hand, the exclusive appointment of career judges might have led to conflicting narrow, parochial attitudes among the justices with the result that some of the judgments might have represented merely compromises between national legal doctrines and traditions.[2] Nevertheless, experience on the bench cannot be wholly disregarded as an important qualification for the justices of the Court. The ideal composition of the Court of the European Communities might be a mixture of both career judges and men with a thorough legal background that have had experiences and proven themselves competent in high positions in administration, business, and the labor movement.

Since the advocates-general are a significant aid to the Court in arriving at a fair and just decision, a brief description of their backgrounds is essential for a full appreciation of the Court.

The educational and occupational backgrounds of the two advocates-general mirror those of the judges of the Court. Both have a formal legal education. Mr. Lagrange pursued an administrative and judicial career in the highest administrative court in France, the Council of State (*Conseil d'Etat*). During this career,

---

lawyers who are strangers to the real world, but of men who are familiar with actual conditions and who recognize the common interest of the European workers." (*Verhandlungen des deutschen Bundestages*, 1951–52, p. 7712.)

[1] In many decisions the Court has used the purposes of the Treaties as an important aid in the interpretation of their provisions. See p. 39, *infra*.

[2] See Riese, *op.cit.*, p. 273.

he held, among others, the position of government commissioner and finally became a member of the court. He also participated as a legal expert in the negotiations which resulted in the signing of the Treaty establishing the Coal and Steel Community and has been a prolific writer and commentator on this subject.

Mr. Roemer's background is quite different. Besides being trained as a jurist, he also engaged in the study of economics and political science. He has had some experience on the bench, but most of his legal career was devoted to the practice of law. In addition, Mr. Roemer held important positions in the banking field and was a member of an economic study group which was charged by the West German government with the task of developing plans for economic reorganization and monetary reform after World War II.

Finally, a few words about the registrar of the Court, who, as has been shown earlier, performs important functions in the operations of the Court. Mr. Albert van Houtte also has served from the beginning of the Court of Justice until the present. He is a Belgian, who holds a doctor of law degree and a degree in political and social economy from the University of Louvain. His major interest until his appointment as registrar of the Court appears to have been in the field of agriculture. Before World War II he held a high post with the Belgian Ministry of Agriculture and since 1946 he has occupied important positions with the European offices of the Food and Agricultural Organization of the United Nations. He thus represents the same broad legal, administrative, and economic interests as are reflected in the composite background of the judges of the Court.

CHAPTER III

THE JURISDICTION OF THE COURT

As has been mentioned earlier, the jurisdictional powers of the Court of the European Communities are extensive and exceed those normally possessed by an international tribunal in the traditional sense. The provisions granting jurisdiction to the Court are scattered throughout the Treaties underlying the three Communities, the Conventions on the Statute of the Court, the Protocols on the Privileges and Immunities of the Communities, the personal statutes of the Communities, and other regulations implementing the Treaties.

The Court of Justices has exclusive jurisdiction for the settlement of disputes between the Member States regarding the interpretation and application of the three Treaties. The governments of the Member States are under obligation not to submit such a dispute to any other international tribunal such as, for instance, the International Court of Justice at the Hague.[1]

Access to the Court

In keeping with the wide and varied jurisdiction, which the Court is allowed to exercise, access to it in terms of plaintiffs and defendants is not limited only to states which under the classic concepts of public international law alone possess "full procedural capacity before international tribunals." [2] On the contrary, actions can also be brought before the Court by the major organs of the Communities, namely, the Commissions, the High Authority, the Council of Ministers, and the Parliament as well as by the Board of Directors of the European Investment Bank. Moreover,

[1] Articles 219 EEC Treaty, 193 Euratom Treaty, and 87 ECSC Treaty. The latter provision is somewhat narrower in its wording.

[2] L. Oppenheim, H. Lauterpacht, *International Law* (London, 1955), p. 20.

private persons, natural or legal, and private enterprises are permitted to file suits with the Court under certain conditions. Professor Donner, currently the president of the Court, has pointed to the justice of this arrangement in a recent article. He stated that as long as the executive bodies of the Communities are authorized to "by-pass the governments and administrations of the Member States and to address their regulations and decisions directly to the national subjects, it is meet that those persons should in their turn be entitled to lodge an appeal against those acts with the Court." [1] In this connection it should be stressed that not only businessmen or business enterprises affected by the provisions of the Treaties can bring action, but also civil servants of the Communities and third parties who have suffered damages through acts of the Communities.

The organs of the Communities authorized to bring actions before the Court, the Member States, and private parties may also be defendants to a suit although the possibility of bringing a suit against private parties is quite restricted.[2] In addition, the Court itself may be sued in civil service matters, and such a suit has actually been brought against the Court and was held admissible.[3] Finally, the Board of Governors of the European Investment Bank may be made a defendant in an action in which the legality of a resolution of that body is questioned by the government of a Member State, the EEC Commission, or by the Board of Directors of the Bank.[4]

---

[1] A. M. Donner, "The Court of Justice of the European Communities," *The Record of the Association of the Bar of New York* (May 1962), pp. 232–243, p. 235. See also articles 33–38, 40–43 ECSC Treaty, 169–171, 173, 175, 178–180 EEC Treaty, 141–144, 145, 148, 151, 152 Euratom Treaty.

[2] Examples may be found in articles 145(2) Euratom Treaty and 40(2) ECSC Treaty.

[3] Gabriel Simon v. Court of Justice of the European Communities, Dec. No. 15/60, June 1, 1961, 7 Rec. 223 (1961). It is interesting to note that the claim of the plaintiff was upheld in the decision.

Despite the wording of articles 175 EEC Treaty and 148 Euratom Treaties that "other institutions" of the Communities may refer violations of the Treaties to the Court of Justice, it has not been considered possible that the Court as "another institution" could bring action "ex officio." (See Wohlfarth-Everling-Glässner-Sprung *op.cit.*, p. 495, comment 1 to article 175).

[4] Article 180 (b) EEC Treaty.

Classification of Jurisdictional Powers

The extensive jurisdictional powers of the Court of the European Communities defy precise categorization. Yet, for the purpose of illustration and possibly for a better understanding of the nature of the Court, it seems to be useful to identify four broad categories of jurisdictional powers although it should be understood that these categories do not cover all of the Court's competences.

Since the origins, powers, and objectives of the Communities are to be found in international treaties, and since the Communities as international organizations possess international personality and are subjects of international law,[1] one may assume with some justification that the Court has the character of an international tribunal. However, while the Court has indeed been given the competence to act as an international tribunal, this role so far has not been prominent because most problems that have arisen between the Member States have been solved by negotiation. Much more significant has been the Court's role as a constitutional and, especially, as an administrative tribunal. In addition, the Treaties have in certain specified cases conferred upon the Court civil jurisdiction in a common law sense.[2] These four broad categories will be examined in this order below; their examination will be followed by a brief description of those miscellaneous

[1] Articles 6 ECSC Treaty, 210 EEC Treaty, and 184 Euratom Treaty.

[2] Cf. E. Stein, "The New Institutions" in E. Stein and T. L. Nicholson, eds., *American Enterprise in the European Common Market, A Legal Profile* (Ann Arbor, Mich., 1960), pp. 70–71, and Bächle, *op.cit.*, pp. 19–23. Advocate-General Maurice Lagrange in "La Cour de Justice de la CECA," *Revue du Droit Public et de la Science Politique* (1954), pp. 417–435, distinguishes only between two broad categories, namely the competences of an administrative and of a constitutional court. M. A. van Houtte, the registrar of the Court, in ' La Cour de Justice de la Communauté Européenne du Charbon et de l'Acier," *European Yearbook*, Vol. II, pp. 183–222, considers the Court to have the competences of an international, constitutional, and administrative Court (pp. 187–196). See also Bebr, *Judicial Control* p. 22 and Wohlfarth *et al.*, *op.cit.*, p. 473 (*Preliminary comments*, No. 3 before article 164) who have similar categories to those presented in the text. See further Valentine, *op.cit.*, pp. 65–69 and Hans-Wolfram Daig, ' Die Gerichtsbarkeit der Europäischen Wirtschaftsgemeinschaft und der Europäischen Atomgemeinschaft," *Archiv des Öffentlichen Rechts* (1958), pp. 132–208, who analyze the competence of the Court in great detail, but do not establish any broad categories of jurisdiction.

assignments which may assume some measure of significance in the foreseeable future.

A. THE COURT AS AN INTERNATIONAL TRIBUNAL

Under the ECSC Treaty, any dispute among Member States concerning the application of the Treaty, that cannot be settled by another procedure provided for in that Treaty, may be submitted to the Court at the request of one of the States which are parties to the dispute.[1] Such a general clause has been omitted from the EEC and Euratom Treaties. Under these Treaties a Member State can bring such a dispute before the Court only if it is alleged that another Member State has violated a Treaty obligation. Moreover, the matter must first be referred to the Commission which must ask the States concerned for their comments and then issue a "reasoned opinion" on the matter. Only after the Commission has given its opinion or if it fails to issue an opinion within a period of three months, is the way open for a Member State to submit the matter to the Court.[2]

The Court may also be asked to arbitrate in any dispute between Member States concerning the object or purpose of the Treaties if such a dispute is submitted to it under the terms of an arbitration clause or *compromis*.[3] In such a case, of course, no preliminary proceedings of the Commission are required. On the other hand, arbitration cannot be requested in cases where a Treaty violation on the part of a Member State is alleged since such disputes are governed by the specific rules discussed in the previous paragraph.[4]

In connection with the above provisions, it is important to remember that the Member States have obligated themselves not to submit any dispute regarding the application and interpre-

[1] Article 89(1).

[2] Articles 170 EEC Treaty and 142 Euratom Treaty. Exceptions to the rule of referring a matter first to the Commission are found in articles 225(2) EEC Treaty and 38(3) Euratom Treaty because of a need for a speedy and final decision. For more details see Daig, *op.cit.*, pp. 190, 191.

[3] Articles 89(2) ECSC Treaty, 182 EEC Treaty, and 170 Euratom Treaty.

[4] Cf. Daig, *op.cit.*, p. 202 and Bächle, *op.cit.*, p. 16.

tation of the Treaties to any tribunal, except the Court of the European Communities. As a consequence, the International Court of Justice at the Hague is excluded from any jurisdiction over disputes concerning the Treaties. It should be noted that the jurisdiction of other courts is excluded only in disputes between Member States. In disputes regarding the application and interpretation of the Treaties involving private parties national courts may also be competent.[1]

B. THE COURT AS A CONSTITUTIONAL TRIBUNAL

If one considers that the constitution of a state outlines the framework and functions of its major governmental organs and often defines the fundamental goals of the state, one is justified to view the Paris and Rome Treaties as the fundamental law, the "constitution," of the three Communities. These treaties form the juridical basis for the various Community organs and delineate the basic goals of the Communities. Beyond that, they regulate the relationship of the Communities to the Member States, stipulating the powers and obligations which the organs of the Communities have in relationship to the governments of the Member States and specifying the competences and duties that the Member States have toward the organs of the Communities. From this point of view, one may be permitted to speak of a federal-type structure of the European Communities, and since the Court of Justice is under obligation to ensure the observance of law and justice in the interpretation and application of the Treaties, one may compare it to a "federal" constitutional court. In this respect, the Court can be viewed as the supreme arbiter between the central organs of the Communities and the governments of the Member States, the guardian of the common interests, and the guarantor of the national prerogatives.[2]

---

[1] For more information on this subject, see pp. 54–60 *infra*.

[2] Pierre Pescatore, *La Cour de Justice en tant que juridiction fédérale et constitutionelle*, paper presented at the Cologne Conference "Ten Years of Jurisprudence of the Court of Justice of the European Communities" April 24–26, 1963. See also Stein, *op.cit.*, p. 70.

Although much of the litigation before the Court has been concerned with technical and administrative matters in the field of economics, the Court has had the opportunity on a number of occasions to declare itself on questions regarding the nature and basic goals of the Treaties. On one of these occasions Advocate-General Lagrange referred to the ECSC Treaty as "the charter of the Community" [1] and the Court in its judgment in the same case used the term "constitutionality" when discussing the conformity of quasi-legislative regulations with the provisions of that Treaty.[2] On other occasions the Court has developed the notion of the fundamental objectives of the Treaties by placing particular weight upon the principles found in the opening articles of the three Treaties. In his conslusions during an early case, Mr. Lagrange, speaking of the "philosophy of the ECSC Treaty," pointed out that "it was necessary to examine the question in litigation in relationship to the Treaty as a whole." And later he stated: "What then is the objective of the Treaty? To create a common market of coal and steel, to define the operating rules of this market, and, finally, to organize an institutional system adequate to ensure its operation."[3]

The Court has followed Mr. Lagrange in his emphasis upon the importance of the statements of principles found in the opening paragraphs of the Treaties in a number of judgments. In an early decision, it stated that "the articles 2, 3, and 4 of the ECSC Treaty constitute the fundamental provisions establishing the common market and the common objectives of the Community."[4] Later decisions have affirmed this position of the Court [5] and in a recent judgment in 1963 the Court has applied similar concepts to an interpretation of the EEC Treaty.[6]

---

[1] Fédération Charbonnière de Belgique v. High Authority, Dec. No. 8/55, July 16, 1956, 2 Rec. 199 (1955–56) at p. 263.

[2] *Ibid.*, p. 227.

[3] Government of the French Republic v. the High Authority, Dec. No. 1/54, December 21, 1954, 1 Rec. 7 (1954–55), p. 232.

[4] *Ibid.*, p. 23.

[5] For example Royal Government of the Netherlands v. High Authority, Dec. No. 6/54, March 21, 1955, 1 Rec. 201 (1954–55), p. 232.

[6] Request for a Preliminary Decision in the Case of Van Gend & Loos v. The Fiscal

The Powers of the Communities' Organs

The Treaties bestow upon the Court the responsibility of reviewing the lawfulness of the acts of the other major organs of the Communities.[1] In this respect the Court may be viewed as exercising the control functions of a constitutional court under a constitution based on the principle of the separation of powers. However, the jurisdictional powers of the Court in this role are not unlimited; rather, they are circumscribed in detail and their latitude varies between the ECSC Treaty on the one hand and the Rome Treaties on the other.

Under all three Treaties the Court has jurisdiction over appeals of a Member State or the Council of Ministers claiming that an act of the High Authority or of the Commissions should be annulled on the grounds of legal incompetence, major violations of procedure, infringement of the Treaties or of any legal provision relating to their application, or abuse of powers. These are the same four grounds upon which administrative acts may be challenged before the French *Conseil d'Etat*, France's highest administrative court. These grounds will be discussed in greater detail later under the section of the Court's administrative competences.[2]

The Rome Treaties permit the Commissions and a Member State to make a similar appeal to the Court also against the acts of the Council of Ministers, but other organs of the two Communities such as the Parliament or a third state are not able to lodge this appeal.[3] On the other hand, under the ECSC Treaty, a more limited appeal is available for the High Authority or a

Administration of the Netherlands, Dec. No. 26–62, February 5, 1963, 9 Rec. 1 (1963) at pp. 22, 23.

[1] Articles 33–34 and 38 ECSC Treaty, 173–176 EEC Treaty, and 146–149 Euratom Treaty.

[2] Some authors, for instance Wohlfahrt *et al.*, *op.cit.*, comment 3 before Article 164, consider the Court's jurisdiction in these cases as falling within the category of administrative court functions. However, in this writer's opinion, the Court is involved in administrative jurisdiction only when it hears complaints of private parties against administrative acts of the Community organs. In agreement Stein, *op. cit.*, at p. 70 and Peter Hay, "Federal Jurisdiction of the Common Market Court," *American Journal of Comparative Law* (1963), pp. 21–40.

[3] Article 173 EEC Treaty and 146 Euratom Treaty.

Member State to request the Court to anull a resolution of the Parliament or the Council. Such an appeal, however, may be made only on the grounds of legal incompetence or major violations of procedure.[1]

The EEC and Euratom Treaties also allow an appeal against inaction of the Commissions or the Council of Ministers in cases where the Treaties require an action by these organs. These appeals aiming at a declaration by the Court that the Treaty has been violated may be lodged by a Member State or by "the other institutions of the Community" which presumably includes the Parliament.[2] Under the ECSC Treaty, however, an appeal to the Court can be made only against inaction of the High Authority, and only by a Member State or the Council of Ministers.[3]

If the Court declares the failure to act as being contrary to the provisions of the Treaties, the organs involved must take the measures required for the implementation of the judgment of the Court. Similarly, if the Court declares an act of an organ of the Communities null and void, the institution from which the act originated is obligated to take new measures in accordance with the judgment of the Court.[4]

A final difference between the Paris and Rome Treaties pertains to the extent of the Court's review powers. Under the ECSC Treaty, the Court cannot review the High Authority's evaluation of economic facts and circumstances upon which the promulgation of a certain act was based. This restriction, however, can be disregarded when the High Authority is alleged to have abused its powers or to have clearly misinterpreted a provision of the Treaty or of a rule of law relating to its application.[5] In the Common Market and Euratom Treaties this re-

---

[1] Article 38 ECSC Treaty.
[2] Articles 175, EEC Treaty and 148 Euratom Treaty. The Court, however, can not be included under the phrase "other institutions," as this would mean an involvement *ex officio*. See Wohlfahrt *et.al.*, *op.cit.*, comment 1 to Article 175 and Bebr, *Judicial Control*, *op.cit.*, pp. 122–123. Of a different opinion is Daig, *op.cit.*, p. 178.
[3] Article 35.
[4] Articles 34 ECSC Treaty, 176 EEC Treaty nad 149 Euratom Treaty.
[5] Article 33(1).

strictive phrase has been omitted entirely, leaving it to the Court to decide on the extent of its review in a specific case.[1]

It is noteworthy that the Treaties do not provide the means for the organs of one Community to lodge appeals against the organs of another Community. Especially, as the Common Market and the Atomic Energy Community expand, one can envision conflicts of competences with the Coal and Steel Community in such fields as anti-trust and social law. To have the facility of calling upon the Court for a decision in such a conflict seems to be most desirable and it is hoped that this *lacuna* may be filled in a future treaty revision.

Although constitutions of states attempt to define the powers of their governmental organs and seek to prescribe areas of authority and responsibility for these organs, time and changing conditions often reveal gaps which must be bridged by the courts if the constitutional edifice is to meet the challenges of the day. The jurisprudence of the United States Supreme Court is the best evidence of the continuing constitutional challenges with which that Court has been faced since its inception. In a similar vein, the Court of the European Communities had to concern itself with the extent of the powers conferred upon the organs of the Communities by the Treaties and with the interrelationship existing between the organs of each of the Communities.

With regard to the power that may be exercised by an organ of the Communities, the Court was confronted with several cases in which it had to determine the extent of the powers possessed by the High Authority. The first case concerned a dispute between the *Fédération Charbonnière de Belgique* and the High Authority in which a gradual reduction of coal prices was in question. The Belgian Coal Federation alleged that the Coal and Steel Treaty had envisaged a market in which the enterprises would be free to fix the prices and that any intervention by the High Authority

[3] Bebr, *Judicial Control, op.cit.*, p. 88 states that "on several occasions the Court found it necessary, and quite justifiably so, to examine and review economic findings even in instances not expressly provided for by the ECSC Treaty," meaning article 33(1). On the other hand, the Court must be aware of its judicial function and must not assume the functions of the administrator.

had to be limited to those cases expressly provided for in the Treaties. As a consequence, the Court held that since no express powers permitted direct action by the High Authority to fix reduced prices, such powers must of necessity be implied. The Court stated that the Treaty imposed upon the High Authority the obligation to realize the objectives fixed by the Treaty and that therefore the High Authority must have not only the power, but also the obligation to take the measures necessary to implement the goals of the Treaty. The Court based its holdings on the principles of municipal and international law according to which the rules established by a law or an international treaty imply those rules without which the rules expressly established would make no sense or would not permit a reasonable or useful application.[1]

It should be noted that the Court has formulated only a limited and rigidly circumscribed doctrine of implied powers. There is no attempt to impute a new power to the Community organs. Powers can only be implied to implement a power already expressed in the Treaty and then only to achieve the limited purpose of that express power and to accord it a reasonable and useful application. In addition, the utilization of the principle of implied powers is severely restricted under the EEC and Euratom Treaties by provisions which expressly confer upon the Council of Ministers a certain "gap-filling" power. These provisions authorize the Council, by accepting unanimously a proposal of the Commission, to enact measures for the furtherance of the aims of the Community in those cases where the Treaty has not provided for the requisite powers of action.[2]

---

[1] Fédération Charbonnière de Belgique v. High Authority, Dec. No. 8/55, November 29, 1956, 2 Rec. 302 (1955–56) pp. 304–5. In two later cases, the Court again referred to the doctrine of implied powers, but the Court held in these cases that it could not derive an implied power for the High Authority from the text or spirit of the Treaty. (Government of the Italian Republic v. High Authority, Dec. No. 20/59, July 15, 1960, 6 Rec. 665, p. 686, and Government of the Kingdom of the Netherlands v. High Authority Dec. No. 25/29, July 15, 1960, 6 Rec. 723 [1960] p. 757.) See also the critical comments of Advocate-General Maurice Lagrange in "Les Pouvoirs de la Haute Autorité et l'application du Traité de Paris," *Revue du Droit Public et de la Science Politique*, January–February 1961, pp. 40–58, particularly 46–48.

[2] Articles 235 EEC Treaty and 203 Euratom Treaty. Some writers hold that these

While the doctrine of implied powers is of course well known in American constitutional law,[1] it is interesting to note that some international organizations also require a certain measure of implied powers in order to discharge their functions effectively. Such has been the experience of the International Labor Organization, the International Monetary Fund, and the United Nations. The International Court of Justice at The Hague recognized this by stating that the United Nations must be deemed to have those powers which, though not expressly provided in the Charter, are conferred upon it by necessary implication as being essential to the performance of its duties.[2]

The constitutional problem of delegation of power, faced by the U.S. Supreme Court on several occasions,[3] has also confronted the Court of the European Communities. A rather interesting case concerned the attempt by the High Authority to delegate certain of its powers to an agency in Brussels which had been set up to run a system of subsidies for the purpose of equalizing the cost of scrap iron. The Court held that delegation an unrestricted of powers constituted a violation of the Treaty. However, the Court did envisage that a delegation of powers might be possible provided that it did not upset the carefully balanced institutional structure of the Treaty and that the High Authority would still exercise effective control over the powers delegated. The Court saw in the equilibrium of powers as provided by the institutional structure of the Community a fundamental guaranty accorded by the ECSC Treaty to the enterprises to which the Treaty applied.[4]

Finally, a fairly recent decision of the Court throws an interesting light on the idea of the unity of the three Communities. An official of the High Authority had resigned from his position and

---

provisions exclude entirely the application of the principle of implied powers. See Wohlfahrt, *et. al.*, *op.cit.*, comment 7 to article 235.

[1] McCulloch v. Maryland, 4 Wheat. 316 (1819).

[2] J. F. McMahon, "The Court of the European Communities: Judicial Interpretation and International Organization," *The British Yearbook of International Law* (1961), pp. 320–350, at p. 340.

[3] For example, Hampton Jr. & Co. v. U.S., 276 U. S. 394 (1928).

[4] Meroni & Co., Industrie Metallurgiche, S.P.A. v. High Authority, Dec. No. 9/56 4 Rec. 9 (1958), pp. 40–47.

had taken a post with an institution of the EEC. The official was denied a claim for a separation allowance because the Court recognized a "functional unity" of the three European Communities which did not permit the payment of a separation allowance to an official moving from an institution of one of the Communities to the institution of another of the Communities. The Court followed the conclusions of Advocate-General Roemer, who acknowledged that each of the Communities had its own legal personality, but who emphasized the many links that existed between the Communities. Mr. Roemer stated in this connection that "the European Treaties are nothing else but the partial beginning of a grand general program, dominated by the concept of a complete integration of the European states." [1]

Relations between the Communities and the Member States

It is the legal relationship between the Communities and the Member States which brings most vividly to one's mind the resemblances to a federal structure and it is particularly in disputes between the institutions of the Communities and the governments of the Member States that the Court's jurisdiction may be viewed most clearly as "federal."

The Treaties bestow upon the High Authority and the Commissions certain powers to ensure the fulfillment of the Treaty obligations by the Member States, although considerable differences exist between the procedures and powers provided by the ECSC Treaty on the one hand, and the Rome Treaties on the other. The ECSC Treaty specifies that the High Authority, if it considers that one of the Member States fails to fulfill its obligations under the Treaty, shall take note of such a failure in a "reasoned decision," which allows the State in question a period of time within which to execute its obligations. The State concerned may appeal to the Court, which then rules on the justifi-

---

[1] Alberto Campolongo v. the High Authority, Dec. Nos. 27/59 and 39/59, July 15, 1960, 6 Rec. 795 (1960). In this connection see also Dineke Algera *et al.* v. Common Assembly Dec. Nos. 7/56 and 3–7/57, July 12, 1957, 3 Rec. 81 (1957) in which the Court was faced with the problem of reconciling the principle of the autonomy of a Community's institution with the unity of a Community.

cation of the High Authority's decision. If the appeal is rejected or if no appeal is lodged within two months, certain economic sanctions may be taken by the High Authority acting jointly with the Council of Ministers against the State violating its obligations.[1]

The Rome Treaties provide that the Commissions of the Common Market and Euratom shall in like circumstances address themselves to the governments of the Member States. If a State fails to comply with the request of the Commission to rectify an alleged Treaty violation within a set period, then the Commission may refer the matter to the Court of Justice. In the event that the Court rules against the State and declares that a Treaty violation has been committed, the government of the State involved must take the measures required for the implementation of the judgment of the Court. The Rome Treaties, however, do not permit the application of economic sanctions.[2] Although this may be considered as a backward step from the goal of achieving European political integration, it must not be overlooked that the prospect of creating an unfavorable public image and offending public opinion in the Member States may also serve as a very effective sanction. Certainly, none of the governments of the Member States wishes to be summoned before the Court by either of the Commissions to hear its action or inaction condemned in law.

It is noteworthy that the EEC Commission has already several times used its power to bring before the Court of Justice the governments of Member States which appeared to have violated their obligations under the Treaty. In 1961 two actions were filed against the Italian government; one for restricting the importation of pigs and pork products, and the other for applying to imported radio parts a higher tariff than justified by the tariff in

[1] Article 88 ECSC Treaty. Van Houtte, *op.cit.*, p. 188, considers action under this article as part of the Court's international jurisdiction.

[2] Articles 169, 171 EEC Treaty and 141, 143 Euratom Treaty. Wohlfahrt *et al.*, *op.cit.*, in comments 3a before article 164, appear to consider these provisions to fall under the Court's international jurisdiction. See also article 225 of the EEC Treaty which permits the Commission to appeal immediately to the Court without first consulting the State concerned if the alleged Treaty violation has the effect of distorting conditions in the Common Market.

force on January 1, 1958, the date which was to be used for the calculation of the progressive tariff reductions. A third action was brought in 1962 against the government of Belgium and Luxembourg for levying a higher fee on import licences for gingerbread than was permitted by the "Common Market" provisions of the EEC Treaty. In all three cases, the Court upheld the contentions of the EEC Commission that the actions of the Member States constituted violations of their Treaty obligations. The governments involved promptly complied with the rulings of the Court; as a matter of fact, in the first case against Italy, the government lifted the import restrictions before the Court pronounced its judgment.[1] A fourth case against the German Federal Republic for placing unwarranted restrictions on the importation of beef was dropped by the EEC Commission in April of 1962 after the Federal government had rectified the alleged violation of the Treaty. Still pending are two cases initiated very recently by the EEC Commission against the governments of Belgium and Luxembourg for charging an unwarranted fee for the issuance of import licenses for certain dairy products.[2]

The cases mentioned above are not the only ones in which barriers have been erected by the governments of the Member States to impede the flow of goods across national frontiers in contravention of the EEC Treaty. The number of obstacles to trade, which could be considered as possible Treaty violations, reached 150 early in 1963,[3] an indication that interest groups had been quite successful in putting pressure on the six governments for the inauguration of protectionist measures. The EEC Commission has settled many of these cases out of court and has resorted to the institution of suits only in cases where the maintenance of general principles was involved. It seems only

---

[1] EEC Commission v. the Government of the Italian Republic, Dec. No. 7/61, December 19, 1961, 7 Rec. 633 (1961); EEC Commission v. the Government of the Italian Republic, Dec. No. 10/61, February 27, 1962, 8 Rec. 1 (1962); and EEC Commission v. the Grand Duchy of Luxembourg and the Kingdom of Belgium, Dec. No. 2 and 3/62, December 14, 1962, 8 Rec. 413 (1962).

[2] Cases 90/63 and 91/63, October 15, 1963.

[3] *Time*, February 22, 1963, p. 87.

reasonable to assume that the threat of Court action and the decisions rendered so far by the Court have materially strengthened the hands of the Commission in dealing with these violations of the Treaty.

One may raise the question why some of the governments of the Member States have permitted the rather obvious violations of the Treaty to reach the litigation stage before the Court. Advocate-General Lagrange no doubt characterized these cases accurately when he stated in the opening sentence of his "conclusions" in the first Italian case that it did not involve any difficult legal questions.[1] Two explanations for allowing these cases to be submitted to the Court are possible. First, strong national interest groups may have pressured the government to institute certain protective measures for a particular industry or agricultural commodity and the government concerned wanted the supranational Court to be the scapegoat for the rescission of these measures. In such a case the government may have considered an accommodation to these groups as more important than the unfavorable impression that would be created in the other Member States and possibly to some extent in its own country, by an adverse judgment of the Court. Second, there may have been strong dissension in the cabinet of one of the Member State's government regarding a proposed protective measure which could constitute a Treaty violation, and the cabinet may have wanted the Court to become the arbiter in the dispute. Domestic political considerations obviously also played a prominent role in these circumstances.

Disputes involving the relationship between the Communities and the Member States can also be brought before the Court by the Member governments which have on several occasions instituted actions against the High Authority and the EEC Commission on the grounds that the decisions of these organs had been legally defective.[2] The clash of conflicting economic interests between some of the Member States gave rise to an interesting

[1] Dec. No. 7/61, December 19, 1961, 7 Rec. 633 (1961) p. 663.
[2] See pp. 40–41 *supra*.

litigation in which the High Authority's power to ensure compliance with the Treaty obligations by the Member governments was involved.[1] The litigation, resulting in several decisions by the Court, grew out of the very favorable special rates which the German railroads traditionally allowed for the transport of coal to certain German blast furnaces that were located far from the coal mines. The Lorraine steelworks, which depend on Ruhr coal, benefitted from this practice when they belonged to Germany, but upon their return to France after World War I, they had to pay the much higher regular transport rates for Ruhr coal. Since the ECSC Treaty provides for the abolition of all discrimination in transport rates within the territory of the Community and stipulates that special rates were only to be allowed with the consent of the High Authority, this institution decided to disallow part of the existing German rates but to permit the continuance of others for a variety of reasons. Following this decision of the High Authority, the Court was swamped with appeals against it-appeals from the German government and German industries that the decision was being too rigid, and appeals from the French government and French industries that it was being too soft. The Court, however, basically upheld the decision of the High Authority, although it did disallow two more of the special rates following the French recommendations. Subsequent to the pronouncement of the Court's judgments, the German government reconsidered its entire freight rate structure and introduced a general low rate for coal which was to be applicable to both internal and international traffic.

In late 1962 and early 1963 Germany and Italy became the first Member States to lodge complaints with the Court against decisions of the EEC Commission. Germany claimed that quotas granted for the import of raw materials for the manufacture of

---

[1] See Government of the Federal Republic of Germany v. the High Authority, Dec. No. 3/58, March 8, 1960, 6/I Rec. 117 (1960) and Dec. No. 19/58, May 10, 1960, 6/I Rec. 469 (1960); also Barbara Bergbau *et al.* v. the High Authority, Dec. Nos. 3-18/58, 25 & 26/58, May 10, 1960, 6/I Rec. 367 (1960) and Chambre syndicale de la siderurgy de l'Est de la France *et al.* v. the High Authority, Dec. Nos. 26 & 36/58, May 10, 1960, 6/II Rec. 573 (1960).

brandy and for the import of oranges from countries outside the Common Market had been insufficient and that the customs tariff for the import of oranges from third countries as set up by the Commission was too high. Italy asserted that the Commission had unduly impeded the export of Italian refrigerators to France.

In a judgment delivered in July 1963, the Court sustained the claim of the German government in the brandy case and thus rendered the first decision unfavorable to the EEC Commission.[1] It should be noted, however, that the judgment in this case was based primarily on procedural grounds and did not reflect on the Commission's evaluation of the economic factors involved. In the two other cases, the Commission was sustained as having acted fully within its competence.[2] In the judgment regarding the import of oranges the Court held that the Commission when making decisions is not restricted to consider only factors advanced by the Member governments, but is authorized and required to take into consideration all factors relevant to the situations regardless of whether or not they have been raised by the governments of the Member States. In the refrigerator decision, the Court held that the temporary measure of the Commission allowing France to restrict the import of Italian refrigerators was well founded and justified under article 226 of the EEC Treaty. This article permits Member States during the transitional period to ask the Commission for authorization to take measures of safeguard if one of their economic sectors is in serious difficulties.

A special role as arbiter between the economic interests of the Coal and Steel Community and of one or more of the Member States is assigned to the Court by the ECSC Treaty. If a Member State considers that in a given case an action of the High Authority, or its failure to act, is of such a nature as to provoke fundamental and persistent disturbances in the economy of that

---

[1] Federal Republic of Germany v. EEC Commission, Dec. No. 24/62, July 4, 1963, 9 Rec. 129 (1963).

[2] Federal Republic of Germany v. EEC Commission, Dec. No. 34/62, July 15, 1963 9 Rec. 269 (1963); and Government of the Italian Republic v. EEC Commission, Dec. No. 13/63, July 17, 1963, 9 Rec. 335 (1963).

State, it may request the High Authority to take necessary measures to correct such a situation. In the event that the High Authority fails to take appropriate measures or if the measures taken are inadequate, the Member States may lodge an appeal with the Court which in such a case is authorized to review the cogency and expediency of the High Authority's decisions.[1] According to the Court, the main purpose of this provision "is to establish a balance between the interests of a Member State, whose economy is affected or threatened by fundamental or persistent disturbances, and the general interests of the Community.[2] Because of the extensive review power of the Court in this instance, the authority of the Court exceeds normal judicial control and approaches political control.[3]

One of the many problems pertaining to the relationship between the Federal government and the states which the U.S. Supreme Court was called upon to solve involved the question as to whether a state could impose its income tax on an official of the Federal government.[4] An interesting case dealing basically with the same problem was brought before the Court of the European Communities in 1960.[5]

The civil servants of the Communities enjoy in the territory of each Member State certain privileges and immunities which include exemption from national taxes on salaries, wages or emoluments paid to them by the Communities.[6] The wife of an ECSC official of Belgian nationality had a separate, taxable

[1] Article 37; see also article 226 EEC Treaty which has a similar prupose but is much more restricted in its application.

[2] Niederrheinische Bergwerks-Aktiengesellschaft *et al.* v. High Authority, Dec. Nos. 2 and 3/60, July 13, 1961, 7 Rec. 261 (1961), at p. 288.

[3] Bebr, *Judicial Control, op.cit.*, p. 151.

[4] Graves v. O'Keefe, 306 U.S. 466 (1939).

[5] Jean E. Humblet v. the Belgian State, Dec. No. 6/60, December 16, 1960, 6/II Rec. 1125 (1960).

[6] Article 12 of the Protocol on the Privileges and Immunities of the EEC and Euratom Treaties, and article 11, Protocol of the ECSC Treaty. The civil servants of the Communities, however, now pay to the Communities a relatively small tax which has been imposed under the authority of the same article. For further details regarding the personnel administration of the Communities see Werner Feld, "The Civil Service of the European Communities: Legal and Political Aspects," *Journal of Public Law* (Vol. 12, 1963), pp. 68–85.

income in Belgium. The Belgian Internal Revenue Service requested the ECSC official to declare his income from the Community so that the Belgian authorities could determine the combined income of husband and wife for the purpose of assessing the latter's tax. Although the dispute affected primarily a Belgian national and his government, the Court declared itself competent to hear the case brought by the ECSC official against the Belgian State. It based its stand on the Protocol on Privileges and Immunities which provides that any dispute concerning the interpretation and the application of the Protocol shall be submitted to the Court of the European Communities.[1] As to the substance of the litigation, the Court held that none of the Member States was permitted to take any measure which would constitute a direct or indirect tax levy on the salaries paid by the Communities to its civil servants. These salaries must not even be taken into account when determining the rate applicable to other incomes, such as that of the official's wife. As a consequence, the actions of the Belgian Internal Revenue Service infringed on the ECSC official's rights created by the Protocol on the Privileges and Immunities of the ECSC Treaty. The Court stated that it was powerless to interfere in the Belgian administration or legislature to enforce its judgment and that all it could do was to declare an administrative or legislative act of a Member State to be a contravention of the Community law. The Court pointed out, however, that the Belgian government had obligated itself in the ECSC Treaty to abide by the decisions of the Court [2] and that therefore it should rectify the effects of its illegal actions. The Belgian government complied with the decision of the Court and it is highly significant that, at least so far, no government of the Member States has considered it prudent to defy the opinions of the Court.

It would be erroneous to conclude from the preceding, rather far-reaching decision that the Court might be inclined to enlarge

[1] Article 16 of the ECSC Protocol.
[2] Article 86. See also the similar provisions in articles 5 of the EEC Treaty and 192 of the Euratom Treaty.

its powers beyond the clear provisions of the Treaties.[1] In many of its judgments, the Court has provided evidence of its concern to remain strictly within the letter and the spirit of the Treaties. In this connection it may be well to point to an interesting decision in 1961 in which the Court gave full recognition to the "reserved" powers of the Member States which it called "retained powers." The decision was rendered in a case instituted by a Dutch association of coal mining firms which complained that the High Authority had refused to prohibit a German government subsidy for wages paid to German Coal miners. The plaintiff based its contention upon article 4c of the ECSC Treaty which forbids "subsidies or state assistance.... in any form whatever" by the Member States. The Court sustained the complaint and held that the German laws authorizing the payments to the miners were incompatible with the provisions of the ECSC Treaty and that the High Authority should have taken steps to prohibit the payments. In support of its judgment, the Court elaborated on the distinction between the powers of the Community and the "retained powers" of the Member States as follows:

The Community is founded on a common market, common objectives, and common institutions.... Within the specific domaine of the Community, i.e. for everything which relates to the pursuit of the common objectives within the common market, the institutions [of the Community] are provided with an exclusive authority.... [O]utside of the domaine of the Community, the governments of the Member States retain their responsibilities and [powers] in all sectors of economic policy.... They remain masters of their social policy; the same undoubtedly holds true for large segments of·their fiscal policy.[2]

As a consequence of this decision, the government of the Federal government took steps to amend its laws in order to bring them into agreement with the provisions of the Treaty and the jurisprudence of the Court. This action of the West German government provides an interesting example of the influence

---

[1] The Humblet judgment was not received without criticism. See Pescatore, *op.cit.*
[2] Gezamenlijke Steenkolenmijnen in Limburg v. High Authority, Dec. No. 30/59, February 23, 1961, 7 Rec. 1 (1961), pp. 43–45. See also the pertinent remarks by Roger M. Chevalier in "L'Arrêt 30/59 de la Cour de Justice des Communautés Européennes," *Revue Générale de Droit International Public* (July–September 1962).

which the Court in certain instances is capable of exerting upon the social policies of the Member States, although the Court acknowledges that they "remain masters of their social policy."

Uniform Interpretation of the Treaties

One of the tasks of a supreme court in a federation is to ensure the uniform interpretation of the federal constitutions and federal statutes. If one were to view the Treaties as the constitution of the Communities and the Community law as a legal superstructure over the municipal laws of the Member States, one may say that the Court of Justice has a somewhat similar responsibility regarding the uniform application of the Treaties and of the quasi-legislative pronouncements made by the various Community organs. By virtue of the Treaties' ratification by the Member States many norms contained therein have become an integral part of the municipal law of each Member State and disputes regarding their application and interpretation may fall within the competence of the domestic courts. Enterprises and individuals in the Member States are not only directly subject to the Community jurisdiction, but also remain under the jurisdiction of the Member States. Although in certain matters the Treaties have bestowed upon the Court of Justice exclusive jurisdiction, the domestic courts remain competent in other cases including litigations to which one of the Communities may be a party.[1] Thus the domestic courts of the various Member States have occasion to interpret the Treaties underlying the Communities and have done so in a number of cases.

The interpretive powers of the domestic courts with regard to the Treaties as well as to the statutes and other acts [2] of the

---

[1] Articles 183 EEC Treaty, 155 Euratom Treaty. The ECSC Treaty does not have a similar provision, but the legal situation is assumed to be similar. (See Wohlfahrt *et al., op.cit.*, comment 4 to article 183 and Bebr, *Judicial Control, op.cit.*, pp. 178–180).

[2] Under the Rome Treaties "acts" may be "regulations," "decisions," or "directives." Regulations resemble American statutes inasmuch as they are binding on and directly applicable to private parties in the Member States. On the other hand, a decision binds only the addressee named therein. Finally, directives are addressed and are binding on Member States only; they leave form and means for the achievement of the desired result to the agencies of the Member States. (See article 189

organs of the Communities are not unlimited. In order to prevent six different interpretations and applications of the Treaties and of the acts of the Communities by the national courts which could frustrate the goal of a Common Market under common rules, the Court of the European Communities has been given certain competences in the interest of ensuring uniformity of law. Under the Coal and Steel Community Treaty, the domestic courts are obliged to refer to the Court of Justice any case in which the validity of resolutions of the High Authority or the Council is contested.[1] In other cases the domestic courts are empowered to interpret the ECSC Treaty as well as the statutes and acts of the organs of the Coal and Steel Community without restriction. This *lacuna* has been filled by the Treaties of Rome which provide that whenever questions are raised concerning their interpretation or concerning the interpretation of statutes and acts of the organs of the Communities before a domestic court from whose decision no appeal lies under national law, such a court is obliged to refer the question to the Court of the Communities for its ruling. The preliminary decision of that Court with regard to the interpretation to be adopted must be observed by the domestic court in its judgment in the case before it.[2] While domestic courts of the last resort are obliged to refer questions of interpretation of the Community law to the Court of Justice, lower courts may do the same at their discretion; it should be noted, however, that in such case the ruling of the Court of Justice is also binding. This scheme joins the Court of Justice and the national jurisdictions into a coordinated system for a common purpose. The execution

EEC Treaty and 161 Euratom Treaty; also Wohlfarth *et al.*, *op.cit.*, comment 2 to article 173.) The ECSC Treaty distinguishes between "general" and "individual" decisions which are somewhat similar to the "regulations" and "decisions" of the Rome Treaties. In addition, an "act" may be a "recommendation" which resembles the "directive" of the Rome Treaties except that it may also be addressed to private parties who then will have the choice of means for attaining the desired objectives. (See articles 14 and 33 ECSC Treaty and Bebr. *Judicial Control*, pp. 37–49.)

[1] Article 41. The term "resolution" has been interpreted as including the decisions and directives of the named ECSC organs. See Roger-Michel Chevalier, "Le droit de la Communauté Européenne et les juridictions Françaises," *Revue du Droit Public et de la Science Politique* (1962) pp. 646–663 at p. 660 and Bebr, *Judicial Control*, p. 186.

[2] Articles 177 EEC Treaty and 150 Euratom Treaty.

of this scheme requires, as Advocate-General Lagrange aptly pointed out in his "conclusions" to a recent case, collaboration and mutual respect for the respective competences of the national courts and the Court of the Communities.[1]

A first request for a preliminary decision under the EEC Treaty provisions reached the Court during its 1961–62 term. The request came from the Court of Appeals at the Hague (Netherlands) and pertained to the interpretation of the anti-trust regulations of that Treaty. The case involved the legality of an exclusive export sales contract between the Bosch Co. of Germany, a manufacturer of refrigerators, and the sole distributor for its products in the Netherlands. An independent importer of Bosch refrigerators in Rotterdam, who had been sued by Bosch and his distributor for damages and discontinuance of his import and sales activities, claimed that the exclusive distributor agreement was null and void because it contravened the anti-trust provisions of the EEC Treaty.[2]

In its interpretation of the anti-trust provisions of the EEC Treaty,[3] the Court held that these provisions had been operative in principle since the Treaty had come into force. However, the prohibition of agreements preventing or restricting competition in the Common Market could become fully effective in a particular case only after an authoritative evaluation of each agreement had been made as to whether it was actually contravening the anti-trust regulations of the Treaty. As a consequence, objectionable agreements were not null and void *ab initio*, but required a "reasoned" decision by the authorities of the Member States or the Commission to nullify it.

While from the standpoint or rapid implementation of a freely competitive Common Market this decision of the Court may have appeared as weak, it was a useful and practical decision. An interpretation of the anti-trust provisions of the Treaty which

[1] Request for a Preliminary Decision by the Court of Appeals of the Hague in the case of Kledingverkoopbedrijf Co. de Geus v. (1) Robert Bosch GmbH, (2) Willem van Rijn Inc., Dec. No. 13/61, April 6, 1962, 8 Rec. 89 (1962), p. 115.

[2] *Ibid.*

[3] Cf. articles 85–89 of the EEC Treaty.

would have considered all possibly objectionable agreements null and void would have created a great deal of legal insecurity since some of these agreements might have been found valid later and the problem would have arisen as to whether such validity should have a retroactive effect. While in all likelihood the Court's interpretation of the treaty's anti-trust provisions has prolonged the legal and economic life of cartels actùally incompatible with these provisions, the Court's primary concern had to be the creation of legal stability in the Community – a *sine qua non* for the orderly implementation of the EEC Treaty.

At the time that the Court was occupied with the Bosch decision, the EEC Commission was engaged in drafting implementing regulations for the Treaty's anti-trust provisions. The drafting of these regulations was obviously carried out in cooperation with the Court since they reflect quite accurately the Court's views as evidenced in the Bosch decision. The gist of these regulations, No. 17 to be precise,[1] requires the registration of existing and new cartels with the Commission which will issue a "reasoned" decision as to whether a cartel or agreement falls under the prohibition of the Treaty's anti-trust provisions. By June of 1963, 35,000 cartels and agreements had been registered with the EEC Commission, but not the first decision had been taken regarding their status. There can be little question that when the Commission begins making these decisions, the Court will receive its share of complaints which will burden it with the solution of new and varied legal problems.

The Bosch decision has been acclaimed as one of the most important judgments the Court has rendered. It has clarified the somewhat obscure anti-trust provisions of the EEC Treaty about whose meaning many commentators had argued in many learned articles.[2] But there can also be little doubt that Regulation No. 17 will raise many new questions which will keep the Court occupied

---

[1] For the basic text see *Journal Officiel*, February 7, 1962, pp. 204/62–211/62; the regulation has been amended several times.

[2] See for example Fernand-Charles Jeantet, "Observation sous l'arrêt de la Cour du 6 Avril 1962," *Juris-Classeur Périodique*, No. 24 of June 13, 1962. For a thorough listing of literature see Wohlfarth, *et al., op.cit.* pp. 240, 241.

for many years to come.[1] From this point of view one may well question whether the legal stability which the Court was so intent in creating has been achieved. Many enterprises are not informed much better now than a year ago as to whether or not they fall under the prohibition of the EEC Treaty's anti-trust provisions.

Another preliminary decision by the Court was pronounced in February of 1963. It was based on a request of the Customs Tariff Commission in Amsterdam, an administrative court of the last resort, which asked for an interpretation of article 12 of the EEC Treaty. This article is a key article of the Treaty; it prohibits the introduction of "any new customs duties on importation or exportation or of charges with equivalent effect" and the increase of "such duties or charges" in the commercial relations between the Member States. The case arose from the refusal of a Dutch firm importing chemicals from Germany to pay import duties under a tariff which it considered an increase over a previous tariff applied to the same product.[2]

The Court of the Communities held that article 12 of the EEC Treaty was directly applicable within the municipal law of the Member States and that it created individual legal rights of private persons which had to be observed and safeguarded by the domestic courts of these countries. The Court declared that the EEC Treaty was more than an agreement that created merely mutual obligations between the contracting states. It found this concept confirmed by the preamble of the Treaty which was not only aimed at the governments but also at the people of the Member States. The Court concluded that

the Community constitutes a novel judicial order of international law, in favor of which the States within certain areas have limited their sovereign

---

[1] See also Rudolf von Werdt, "Zur Frage der Anwendung von Art. 85 des EWG-Vertrages auf Individualverträge," *Wirtschaft und Wettbewerb* (September 1962), pp. 583–594; Ernst Wolf, "Zum Kartellrecht der EWG," *Wirtschaft und Wettbewerb* (October 1962), pp. 645–660; and P. Verloren van Thermaat, "Gedanken zur Wettbewerbspolitik im Gemeinsamen Markt," *Wirtschaft und Wettbewerb* (July/August 1963) pp. 555–564.

[2] Request for a Preliminary Decision by the Customs Tariff Commission in Amsterdam in the case of Van Gend & Loos v. the Fiscal Administration of the Netherlands, Dec. No. 26/62, February 5, 1963, 9 Rec. 1 (1963).

rights and of which the subjects are not only the States, but also their citizens.... The Community law, independent of the legislation of the States, is capable of creating rights which enter into the legal system of the States.[1]

This vigorous and progressive decision has been greeted with great enthusiasm not only within the civil service of the Communities, but also by most independent observers.[2] Less enthusiastic apparently were the governments of the Member States. The governments of the Netherlands, Belgium, and Germany expressed their opinions during the proceedings that article 12 should not be considered as directly applicable in the municipal law of the Member States. Underlying these opinions may have been the concern that national judges might be confused as to which provisions of the Treaties represent directly applicable law in the Member States. However, the referral system of such questions to the Court of Justice is always available to the national judge who is unsure about the proper interpretation of any of the Treaties' provisions and desires clarification. So far, unfortunately, national courts have not used the referral system to any great extent; in fact even when a requirement for referral action existed, some courts of the last resort have not complied with it. Up to the writing of these lines only some of the Dutch tribunals and a court each in Luxemborg and in Italy have requested the Court of the Communities for a preliminary ruling; four rulings have been rendered and five cases are still pending.[3] Since the Court has no power to compel referral of a

---

[1] *Ibid.*, p. 23. Pescatore, *op.cit.*, applauds this statement but would have preferred if the Court had omitted the words "of international law," because he views the Community law as a legal order *sui generis*.

[2] For example Fr. Rigaux, *Journal des Tribunaux*, March 17, 1963, pp. 190-2, and Dietrich Ehle in *Neue Juristische Wochenschrift* (1963), pp. 974-6.

[3] Bebr, *Judicial Control*, pp. 195-7, lists a number of cases where German and Dutch courts did not request a preliminary ruling from the Court of Justice although they were obviously required to do so under the terms of the Treaties. It seems that a very recent case before the Court of Appeals of Amiens, France, also should have been referred to the Court of the Communities for a ruling; however, the decision of the Court of Amiens has now been appealed. (Affaire Nicolas et Ste. Maison Brandt, Dec. of May 9, 1963; see also note in *Gazette du Palais*, June 16, 1963, Nos. 163-5.) In one of the last preliminary decisions of the Court, the obligation of national tribunals to refer interpretation questions to it was strongly emphasized in the text of the judgment and in the conclusions of Advocate-General Lagrange. (Request for a

question by a national tribunal, it is hoped that for the sake of the uniform development of the Community law some means will be found to ensure compliance by the national courts with the referral provisions of the Treaties. One solution for this problem might be the passage of appropriate parallel legislation in the Member States.[1]

It is interesting to note that the preliminary decision regarding the interpretation of article 12 was rendered only about a week after France denied Great Britain entry into the Common Market and three weeks after General de Gaulle's famous news conference of January 14, 1963. Since the request for a preliminary ruling by the Court of Justice was made in August of 1962, undoubtedly these events had no bearing on the Court's deliberations. Nevertheless, the fact that the release of this strongly integrationist decision followed so closely the other fateful dates can be assumed to have had a most salutary and stimulating effect on the flagging spirits of many a disappointed and frustrated civil servant of the Communities as well as on many good "Europeans" disgusted and disillusioned by the events of the previous weeks.

Revision of Treaties

The EEC and Euratom Treaties may be revised or amended only by the Governments of the Member States, a procedure in which the Court does not participate at all.[2] While a major revision or amendment of the ECSC Treaty also necessitates agreement by the Member States, this Treaty makes provision for a revision by the Community itself, but only within a strictly

Preliminary Decision by the Customs Tariff Commission in Amsterdam in the case of Da Costa en Schaake N.V. *et al.* v. Fiscal Administration of the Netherlands, Dec. Nos. 28–30.62, March 27, 1963, 9 Rec. 59 [1963].) For other decisions see p. 56, footnote 1 and p. 58, footnote 2, *supra.* The latest preliminary decision is in the case of (1) Internationale Crediet- en Handelsvereniging Rotterdam, (2) Coöperatieve Suikerfabriek en Raffinaderij G. A. Puttershoek v. The Minister of Agriculture and Fisheries, The Hague, Dec. Nos. 73 and 74/63, February 18, 1964 (Mimeographed Advance Copy). The Dutch requests for preliminary rulings pending at present are cases Nos. 75/63, 92/63, and 100/63; the Luxembourg request is case No. 101/63 and the Italian request is case No. 6/64.

[1] See Hay, *op.cit.,* pp. 39 and 40.
[2] Articles 236 EEC Treaty and 204, Euratom Treaty.

limited scope and under the control of the Court.[1] It is called the "small revision" and requires the co-operation of all Community organs. The High Authority may propose such a revision; if supported by a five-sixth vote of the Council, both organs jointly submit the proposed Treaty revision to the Court which examines it as to the law and the facts. The Court renders its opinion after having heard the conclusions of both advocates-general in closed session.[2] If the Court finds the proposed revision within the permitted framework and justified by existing conditions, the proposal for revision is submitted to the Parliament for its final approval. The Parliament may merely approve the revision or reject it; it may not amend or change it.[3] To approve the revision requires a majority vote of three-quarters of the members of the Parliament which must represent two-thirds of its total membership. Upon approval by the Parliament, the revision becomes binding without any ratification by the Member States.

As has been mentioned, the framework within which the Coal and Steel Community itself is permitted to revise the Treaty is quite restricted. Such a revision can be carried out only in the event of unforeseen difficulties in the application of the Treaty or in the case of a profound change in the economic and technical conditions directly affecting the common market for coal and steel. Even if these conditions exist, however, treaty revisions can be made only subject to the following limitations. First, the revision must deal with a modification of the rules governing the exercise of the power of the High Authority that is necessary to remedy the unforeseen difficulties or counteract the effects of the changed economic and technical conditions. Second, the revision must not be of such a nature as to alter or infringe on the basic objectives of the Treaty, and, thirdly, it must not result in an alteration of the existing relationship between the powers of the

[1] Article 95(3) ECSC Treaty.
[2] Articles 108(2) and 107 of the Rules of Procedure of the Court (*Journal Officiel*, January 16, 1960, pp. 17/60–46/60).
[3] Karl Carstens, "Die kleine Revision des Vertrages über die Europäische Gemeinschaft für Kohle und Stahl," *Zeitschrift für ausländisches Recht und Völkerrecht*, (January 1961), pp. 1–37, at p. 8. Carstens discusses in detail the problems involved in the application of article 95(3).

High Authority and those of the other organs of the Community.

The Court has taken very seriously its responsibility of examining the "constitutionality" of proposals for small ECSC Treaty revisions. The first advisory opinion of the Court with regard to a proposed revision was sought in 1959.[1] The purpose of the revision was to bestow upon the High Authority increased powers to grant assistance to individual coal mines, which had been forced, as a result of profoundly changed market conditions, to permanently discontinue, curtail, or alter their activities. After making a very thorough analysis of the provisions for a small revision of the Treaty, the Court added two further limitations to the use of this power by the Community organs. First, the proposed revision must not affect the basic structure of the Treaty; second, it must not alter the relationship between the powers transferred to the Community and those "reserved" for the Member States. In other words, the Court presupposed not only an equilibrium of powers between the institutions of the Communities, but also between the Community and the Member States which must not be modified by the proposed Treaty revision. On the basis of these and other considerations, the Court found the proposed revision of the Treaty to be unacceptable; one of the cogent grounds for the Court's opinion was the fear that the equilibrium of powers envisaged by the Treaty was likely to be compromised because the High Authority's proposed new powers could be used only for the coal industry but not for the steel industry.[2]

The position taken by the Court forced the High Authority and the Council of Ministers to revise their proposal in accordance with the Court's opinion and early in 1960 the Court approved the modified proposal for the revision of the Treaty.[3]

In the summer of 1961 the difficulties of the coal mining industry generated by a highly competitive fuel market led to another

[1] Revision of article 56 ECSC Treaty. See Advisory Opinion of the Court of December 12, 1959, 5 Rec. 551, (1959).

[2] *Ibid.*, pp. 555-562. Carstens does not think that the Treaty offers sufficient support for the additional limitations to the small revision of the Treaty (*op.cit.*, p. 21).

[3] Advisory Opinion or the Court of March 4, 1960, 6/I Rec. 107 (1960).

proposal for Treaty revision, in this case for an amendment of the Treaty's anti-trust provisions. The proposal aimed at a relaxation of the regulations under which the High Authority was empowered to grant exemptions to the general prohibition of cartels and other agreements or practices "tending directly or indirectly, to prevent, restrict or distort the normal operation of competition within the Common Market..." [1]

The Court denied the proposed revision on two grounds. First, it found that the proposed text would have the effect of attributing to the High Authority new powers the limits of which were not clearly and precisely defined and which would go beyond a mere modification of its present powers. Secondly, the Court declared that the proposed revision conflicted with one of the imperative, absolute prohibitions of the Treaty regarding cartels and other market-restricting agreements and practices.[2]

It is interesting to note that the authority of the Court to examine the "constitutionality" of the proposed Treaty revisions is actually more than merely an examination. In refusing a proposed Treaty revision, the Court has an opportunity to suggest the general outlines of a possible revision in the arguments it puts forth for rejecting the submitted proposal. Thus the Court itself formulates, to some extent, the material content of the small Treaty revision.[3]

Miscellaneous Functions of a Constitutional Nature

In two cases the EEC and Euratom Treaties provide for the possibility of a request to the Court of Justice to render an advisory opinion on the compatibility of a contemplated legal act with the Treaties.

The European Economic Community, possessing legal personality and being a subject of international law, is authorized in a number of instances to conclude international agreements with third states and international organizations.[4] Such agreements

---

[1] Article 65(1) ECSC Treaty.
[2] Advisory Opinion of the Court of December 13, 1961, 7 Rec. 505 (1961) pp. 514 ff.
[3] Bebr, *Judicial Control, op.cit.*, pp. 161, 162.
[4] Articles 238 and 228.

are negotiated by the Commission but are actually concluded by the Council of Ministers after the Parliament has been consulted in certain cases. Once concluded, these agreements are binding on the institutions of the Community and the Member States. Prior to the conclusion of such an agreement, the Council, the Commission, or the government of a Member State may request the opinion of the Court as to the compatibility of the proposed agreement with the provisions of the Treaty. The Court renders such an opinion only after it has heard both advocates-general in closed session.[1] If the Court issues a negative opinion, the agreement cannot enter into force. The only possibility of concluding such an agreement then is an amendment of the Treaty by the Member States. In view of the difficulties connected with an amendment of the Treaty and subsequent ratification by the Member States, the organs of the EEC might prefer redrafting the agreement in accordance with the Court's opinion. This clearly illustrates the importance of the Court's preliminary opinion and the influence which it is able to exert upon the foreign relations of the Community.

Although the European Atomic Energy Community may also conclude agreements with third states and international organizations, the Treaty does not provide for a similar preliminary control by the Court as does the EEC Treaty.[2] The rationale for this difference may be that agreements concluded by Euratom do not have the force of binding directly the Member States. However, the Court may be called upon to issue an advisory opinion on the compatibility with the Treaty of an agreement which a Member State intends to conclude with a third country, an international organization, or a national or a third country provided, of course, that such an agreement concerns the field of application of the Euratom Treaty. The Member State contemplating the conclusion of such an agreement must submit the draft of the agreement to the Commission which may raise objections if the draft contains clauses impeding the application

[1] Articles 228 EEC Treaty and 106, 107 of the Rules of Procedure of the Court.
[2] Articles 101 and 206, Euratom Treaty.

of the Euratom Treaty. In such an event, the Member State has a choice. It can either attempt to remove the objections of the Commission, or it can petition the Court for a ruling as to the compatibility of the proposed draft with the provisions of the Treaty. Such a ruling must be given by the Court in "expedited proceedings." If the advisory opinion of the Court is negative, the State can not conclude the agreement unless it has been modified in compliance with the opinion of the Court,[1] again an indication of the Court's importance.

With regard to contracts of a national of a Member State with a third state, with a national of a third state, or with an international organization, the Commission may request the governments of the Member States to be advised of those contracts or agreements which fall within the field of application of the Euratom Treaty. If the Commission finds that such agreements contain clauses "impeding the application of the Treaty," it may also ask the Court for an advisory opinion on their compatibility with the Treaty.[2]

Finally the Court is called upon to play a constitutional role in the appointment of the members of the High Authority. Since the governments of the Member States appoint eight members by "agreement among themselves," [3] the possibility exists that a government uses its veto with respect to some of the nominees of another government so often that the appointment process has come to a *cul-de-sac*. Under certain conditions, therefore, a government of the Member States may refer the problem to the Court which may declare the veto null and void if it considers that the right of veto has been abused.[4]

C. THE COURT AS AN ADMINISTRATIVE TRIBUNAL

The Court's jurisdiction is "administrative" where it affords legal redress to individuals and enterprises praying that administrative acts of the Communities' organs be annulled or

---

[1] Article 103 Euratom Treaty.
[2] Articles 104 and 105 Euratom Treaty.
[3] The ninth member is elected by the other eight. See p. 6, footnote 2, *supra*.
[4] Article 10 ECSC Treaty.

appealling against inaction of these organs in cases where they were obligated under the Treaties to take action. As has been pointed out earlier, the right of access of private parties to the Court – without the need of intervention by their governments – is a necessary corollary to the power of the Communities' institutions to act with direct effect upon these parties. This right marks a radical departure from the international tribunal in the traditional sense and strengthens the public law nature of the Community law.

Appeals by Private Parties

The majority of suits filed with the Court to this day have been complaints brought by individuals and enterprises regarding acts or inactions by the High Authority, and lately about actions of the EEC Commission. As a consequence, the administrative law functions of the Court seem to have assumed greater significance than any other phase of the Court's activities.

The Treaties, again, are not uniform in the protection and legal remedies granted private parties. Under the Rome Treaties, any natural or legal person may appeal to the Court against a decision of the Commission or the Council of Ministers which is either addressed to him, or "which although in the form of a regulation or a decision addressed to another person, is of direct or specific concern to him." [1] Regulations have a quasi-legislative character; they are binding in every respect on and directly applicable to individuals and enterprises in the Member States. On the other hand, a decision binds only the addressee named therein which again may be either an individual or an enterprise.[2]

---

[1] Articles 173 EEC Treaty and 146 Euratom Treaty.

[2] Article 189 EEC Treaty and article 161 Euratom Treaty. In addition to the terms "regulation" and "decision," the EEC and Euratom Treaties also use the terms "directive," "recommendation" and "opinion." Directives are addressed to and are binding on Member States, but leave form and means for the achievement of the desired result to the domestic agencies of the Member States. Recommendations and opinions have no binding force on anybody (*ibid.*). The ECSC Treaty uses some of these terms but their meaning is often different, as is explained in footnote 2, p. 54. The meaning of the term "enterprise" has also been the subject of controversy. For more information on this controversy see Gerhard Bebr, "The Concept of Enterprise under the European Communities," *Law and Contemporary Problems* (Summer 1961), pp. 454–463, and pp. 72–76 *infra*.

Since "any" person may lodge an appeal, it is obvious that this right does not depend on any specific legal status, nationality, or type of activity of the plaintiff. Thus the Court is open to American citizens or companies organized in the United States or to foreign companies controlled by American capital if the rights or interests of such citizens or companies are affected in a manner specified in the Rome Treaties.[1]

The grounds for appeal are the same that have been enumerated earlier as available to the Member States, the Commission or the Council. The first ground is legal incompetence which consists of an action by a Community organ outside the defined limits of its legal power and may perhaps be analogized to the common law concept of *ultra vires*. The second ground consists of a major violation of procedure such as the failure to adopt an administrative act by the requisite number of votes or the failure to give sufficient reasons for an act. This ground for appeal may not only be available in case of a violation of a procedural requirement set forth in the Treaty, but also in case of a violation of the inherent procedural requirement of "fair play" which may be viewed as somewhat similar to the American concept of "procedural due process."[2] The third ground, an infringement of the Treaty or of any legal provision relating to its application such as an implementing regulation, is used to contest an administrative act because of an improper interpretation of the Treaties or regulations or because of complete absence of facts to support the challenged act. This ground has been invoked in many cases before the Court and a considerable amount of jurisprudence has been developed by the Court in this area.[3] Finally, an administrative act may be appealed for what the English text of the Treaties calls "abuse of power." The French text calls it *détournement de pouvoir* which is a wellknown term in French administrative law and is also used in the administrative laws of the other

---

[1] Cf. Eric Stein and Peter Hay, "New Legal Remedies of Enterprises: A Survey" in Stein & Nicholson, *op.cit.*, pp. 459–510.

[2] This concept appears to be supported by Stein and Hay, *op.cit.*, p. 467.

[3] See the citations of cases and literature in *ibid.*, p. 468, footnotes 43 and 44.

Member States. It is applied to a situation in which an organ has exercised its power to achieve an end not envisioned in the grant of power. In an early case, Advocate-General Lagrange lectured the Court at length on the meaning of the term.[1] Later, the term was somewhat enlarged by the Court taking into consideration the German meaning of *Ermessensmissbrauch*, a similar notion as *détournement de pouvoir*.[2] As a consequence, the Court considers it a *détournement de pouvoir* if an organ "by its grave lack of foresight or of circumspection, amounting to a disregard of legal objectives, pursued other aims than those for which the powers were provided for...." [3] It is doubtful whether an administrative act in the United States could be attacked on this basis. "Improper purpose" does not seem to offer a ground for review by United States courts, although such an act might be contested on other grounds such as disregard of the requirements of procedural due process or abuse of discretion.

The grounds for appeal of an administrative act under the ECSC Treaty are the same as those under the Rome Treaties. However, the right of appeal under that Treaty is limited to enterprises engaged in the production of coal and steel within the European territories of the Member States and in certain instances to enterprises regularly engaged in the wholesale distribution of these commodities.[4] Neither the "nationality" of the enterprise nor the domicile or seat of the administration of the corporation to which it belongs is relevant. A coal and steel producing enterprise, not legally independent but located within the Community countries, regardless of who owns or controls it and regardless from where it is directed, is under the competence of the Community and also has the right of appeal.[5]

As in the case of an appeal for annulment by a Member State

---

[1] Associazione Industrie Siderurgiche Italiane-ASSIDER v. High Authority, Dec. No. 3/54, February 10, 1955, 1 Rec. 123 (1954–55) pp. 149–175.

[2] Riese, *op.cit.*, p. 273.

[3] Fédération Charbonnière de Belgique v. High Authority, Dec. No. 8/55, July 16, 1956, 2 Rec. 199 (1955–56), p. 310.

[4] Articles 33(2) and 80.

[5] Bebr, *Judicial Control, op.cit.*, p. 60.

or by the Council, the Court may review the High Authority's evaluation of the situation as based on economic facts and circumstances only when the enterprise involved alleges that the High Authority, when issuing an administrative act, abused its powers or clearly misinterpreted the provisions of the Treaty or a rule of law relating to its application.[1]

There are additional legal differences between the ECSC Treaty on the one hand, and the Rome Treaties on the other, regarding the right of appeal by private parties of an act of the Community organs. While a detailed discussion of these differences would exceed the framework of this book,[2] several points deserve mentioning. First, the distinctions between the various acts of the Community organs appear to be more refined in the Rome Treaties than in the ECSC Treaty, particularly the distinction between what constitutes a "regulation," "decision," and "recommendation."[3] Second, under the ECSC Treaty private parties can appeal any decisions "affecting" them, whereas under the Rome Treaties they can appeal decisions not actually addressed to them only if they are "of direct and specific concern" to them.[4] Third, although appeals against decisions are limited in time, the Rome Treaties provide that the validity of a regulation which has become the subject of a dispute in a legal proceeding before the Court, may be questioned on the same grounds on which a decision can be attacked but without regard to any time limit. The regulation, however, must be of "direct and specific concern" to the party questioning its validity.[5] This additional protection for private parties is proper because since regulations have the

---

[1] Article 33 (1) and (2).

[2] For detailed information cf. Bebr, *Judicial Control, op.cit.* pp. 68–79.

[3] For an explanation of these terms see p. 54, footnote 2 and p. 66, footnote 2.

[4] Articles 33 (2) ECSC Treaty, 173 (2) EEC Treaty and 146 (2) Euratom Treaty.

[5] Articles 184 EEC Treaty and 156 Euratom Treaty. The Court has interpreted the term "direct and specific concern" very narrowly in several recent decisions and has thus reduced the ability of private parties to file appeals liberally against regulations under the Rome Treaty. See f.i. Confédération nationale des producteurs de fruits et légumes *et al.* v. EEC Commission, Dec. Nos. 16 and 17/62, December 14, 1962, 8 Rec. 901 (1962) and Victor J. Stone, "The Court and Anglo-Saxon Law," *European Community* (June, 1963), pp. 8, 9.

nature of general laws, it may be impossible to determine within a short period of time whether a certain regulation is of "direct and specific concern" to an individual or an enterprise. In the event that the Court finds the contested regulation to be legally defective, it cannot annul the regulation, but only declare it "inapplicable." Nevertheless, since the Community institutions and national courts are bound to comply with the legal interpretations of the Court, "inapplicability" appears to be in practice the same as annulment. In contrast to the Rome Treaties, the ECSC Treaty provides for a right of appeal against regulations only on the grounds of "abuse of power," but does not require the criterion of "direct and specific concern" as a basis for a private party's right of appeal.[1]

The Treaties also grant to private persons the right of appeal against inaction of some of the Community organs in those cases where these organs are obligated by the Treaties or by the implementing regulations to act but have failed in this obligation. The possibilities of instituting such an appeal are somewhat greater under the ECSC Treaty than under the Rome Treaties. For an appeal against inaction under the Coal and Steel Community Treaty it is sufficient that the High Authority failed to issue a decision it was obligated to make; or in case of a discretionary competence, that the High Authority's failure to act constituted an "abuse of power." In such an event the omission to act must be brought to the attention of the High Authority and if no action is forthcoming after the end of two months, the appeal may be lodged "before the Court... against the tacit negative decision presumed to result from such failure to act." [2] These provisions have made it possible for those who thought the High

---

[1] Article 33 (2). It should be noted that the Court has claimed on several occasions that the material content of an act and not its form is decisive for the nature of the act. Therefore, an individually binding decision that might be disguised as a not-binding opinion or recommendation (EEC terminology) or was issued in the form of a regulation, can be appealed by a private party as an individual decision. See Fédération Charbonnière de Belgique v. High Authority, Dec. No. 8/55, July 16, 1956, 2 Rec. 201 (1954–55) at p. 225, and the decision cited in the preceeding footnote (Confédération nationale) at pp. 918, 919.

[2] Article 35.

Authority too timid in the use of its powers, to lodge an appeal even for inaction against their own national government.[1]

The EEC and Euratom Treaties authorize private parties to make an appeal not only against inaction of the Commission but also against the Council. This is quite understandable if one remembers that both of these organs must in many cases co-operate in issuing decisions and regulations. However, such an appeal to the Court is permitted only in the case that a Community organ has failed to address a decision to the complaining party and that the inaction is a violation of the Treaty.[2] As a consequence private persons are no longer authorized to appeal about inaction in general, and no action is possible, for example, to bring suit for inaction against the Commission for failing to sue a Member State for violation of its Treaty obligations.

The purpose of an appeal lodged for inaction is to establish the duty of a Community organ to act. If the Court finds that action by the organ is required, the latter must take the measures necessary for the implementation of the judgement. Similarly, in case of annulment of an act of one of the Communities' organs, the institution involved must implement the judgment in accordance with the Court's opinion.[3]

Notable Litigations

The litigations selected for discussion in the following pages have not been chosen because they culminated in judgments that have become legal landmarks, but because they seem to highlight the economic importance of the Court and they are interesting from a political point of view.

Some of the actions brought against the High Authority by the titans of the West European steel and coal industry have involved sums of money running into the millions of dollars. Particularly falling into this category have been cases dealing

[1] Donner, *op.cit.*, p. 236.

[2] Article 175 EEC Treaty and 148 Euratom Treaty.

[3] Articles 176 EEC Treaty, 149 Euratom Treaty, and 34 ECSC Treaty. The latter article also allows an action for damages "if the High Authority fails to take within a reasonable period the measures required to give effect to a judgment of annulment."

with the application of an equalization system for the cost of scrap metal in the steel industry. In order to prevent large price increases of scrap within the territory of the Communities when this commodity was scarce, the High Authority established in 1953 and 1954 a subsidy and compensation scheme which imposed a surcharge on the consumption of scrap metal by the steel producers. The purpose of the scheme was to spread the difference between the price of scrap metal purchased on the world market and that purchased within the Member States to all purchased scrap and thus to equalize the cost of this commodity at an overall level lower that the world market price. When in the 1958 recession world and domestic prices for scrap iron approached equality, the scrap metal equalization fund was discontinued as of early 1959 and the scrap metal market in the Member States was freed.

From the surcharge imposed on the steel producers the High Authority allowed one exception; it exempted the consumption of scrap metal reclaimed by the enterprises from their own steel production.[1] As a consequence of this important exemption which could involve large sums of money, a number of controversies arose as to what was meant by "own" scrap metal. The High Authority considered the term to apply only to the formal ownership of scrap by an enterprise having independent legal personality. On the other hand, it considered as subject to the surcharge the so-called "concern-scrap" which was scrap reclaimed by one legally independent enterprise and supplied to another legally independent enterprise even though the two enterprises were closely tied together by financial, economic, and administrative links. Several large German and French firms appealed to the Court against this interpretation of the High Authority and claimed that the economic concept and not the legal concept of an enterprise was the underlying principle of the Treaty.[2] They

---

[1] Letter from the High Authority to the Joint Bureau of Scrap Consumers, December 18, 1957 (*Journal Officiel*, [1958], p. 45).

[2] Article 80 reads in part as follows: "The term enterprise, as used in this Treaty, refers to any enterprise engaged in production in the field of coal and steel..."

referred to the economic unit formed by these legally independent enterprises and to the close organizational and financial ties existing among them. As a consequence, they argued, even the scrap metal transferred from one of these enterprises to another should be considered as "own" scrap free of surcharge.

The Court, however, rejected the arguments of the large steel concerns. It accepted the legal concept of enterprise as advanced by the High Authority, but it did so only after it had convinced itself that a wider interpretation of the term might have been incompatible with the economic and financial objectives of the scrap metal equalization scheme.[1]

Although the regulations concerning the price equalization measures for scrap metal ceased to be in force with the beginning of 1959, several decisions of the Court during its 1961–62 term dealt with litigations arising from the application of these regulations. Among the actions brought against the High Authority were three suits by the German firms Kloeckner, Hoesch, and Mannesmann.[2] The plaintiffs again attacked the legal concept of the term "enterprise." They asserted that in contrast to other trusts and holding companies they were fully integrated concerns whose subsidiaries lacked every autonomy in the direction and conduct of their economic activities. Policy formulation, management, and financial risk of all subsidiaries were in the hands of the plaintiffs.

Mannesmann, in particular, pointed out that it was placed in a disadvantageous position vis-a-vis its competitors because the cost of each ton of steel produced by it would be at least DM 5.– higher than that produced by a competitor of comparable size whose various subsidiaries might be organized as one legal personality. Over a period of four and one half years, this extra cost of steel would amount to 10 million dollars.

[1] Cf. S.N.U.P.A.T. v. High Authority, Dec. Nos. 32 and 33/58, July 17, 1959, 5 Rec. 275 (1958–59), S.A.F.E. v. High Authority, Dec. No. 42/58, July 17, 1959, 5 Rec. 381 (1958–59) and Phoenix-Rheinrohr *et al.* v. High Authority, Dec. No. 20/58, July 17, 1959, 5 Rec. 163 (1958–59).

[2] Kloeckner-Werke AG and Hoesch AG v. High Authority, Dec. Nos. 17 and 20/61, July 13, 1962, 8 Rec. 615 (1962); and Mannesmann AG v. High Authority supported by Phoenix-Rheinrohr AG, Dec. No. 19/61, July 13, 1962, 8 Rec. 675 (1962).

In its judgments the Court refused to accept the arguments of the plaintiffs and maintained its support of the legal concept of enterprise. The reaction to these judgments in Germany was predominently critical; Professor Donner's picture appeared in the *Spiegel* which also berated the Court for its inability to interpret "correctly" the term enterprise.[1] Other papers joined in this criticism [2] part of which was stimulated by the public relations department of the Mannesmann company.[3] Some of the complaints, however, were not entirely unjustified. In cases involving tens of millions of dollars a court which decides in the first and last instance does not constitute a very satisfactory system of adjudication. No matter how excellent the judges of the Court of the European Communities might be, a two-tier court system would provide an essential safeguard against a possible miscarriage of justice and, at the same time, contribute to higher legal quality. Furthermore, a case in which a major question had been decided by a one-instance Court will become a precedent which the Court most likely will be reluctant to overthrow. Thus, the judgments of the Court become the law of the future.

Regardless of whether or not the criticism was justified, it was obviously directed against the wrong party. The establishment of a second instance into the system of the European Court is not up to the Court itself, but is a task to be undertaken by the Member governments since it would require an amendment of the Treaties. The Court might be the last to object to such a change in procedure.

One of the newspapers stressed that the Federal government, although exercising extreme reserve in the matter, had clearly indicated that "it considered in many cases the jurisprudence of the Luxembourg Court as unsatisfactory." [1] Such criticism is

[1] *Der Spiegel*, September 19, 1962, pp. 38, 39.
[2] See for example *Die Welt*, July 31, 1962, *Europa-Union*, September 14, 1962 and *Frankfurter Allgemeine Zeitung*, September 20, 1962.
[3] A large champagne party was held by the Mannesmann Co. early in September 1962, to which newspaper reporters and members of the Federal government were invited and during which company officials discussed the judgment of the Court.
[4] *Frankfurter Allgemeine Zeitung*, September 20, 1962.

neither improper nor unusual; it represents nothing more than the right of dissent regarding a court decision which may be voiced by a government as well as by an individual. The important point is that the decision of the Court must not be flouted. Southern state governments in the United States have frequently expressed their displeasure with some of the Supreme Court's decisions but they have generally complied with them. Even the central government in the United States has at times disagreed with a decision of the Supreme Court but it has never resorted to outright defiance of its verdict.

There can be little question that the Court's judgments supporting the legal concept of enterprise had placed Mannesmann as well as other large integrated German and French concerns in a competitively disadvantageous position compared to those concerns which were organized as a single legal personality. Indeed, concerns essentially similar in their functional and economic structure were subject to different treatment resulting in arbitrary differences in the cost of steel production. On the other hand, the Court's position was legally and logically supportable and it had the important advantage of establishing a criterion that was easily recognizable, thus contributing to greater legal stability. To saddle the High Authority with the obligation of unravelling in each case the intricacies of the functional and economic structure of a large concern in order to decide whether it was subject to a surcharge, would not only have imposed a tremendous workload on the High Authority, but would also have led to more arguments and confusion than already existed. It also would have possibly jeopardized the whole scheme of equalizing the cost of scrap metal for the entire industry. The best thing, of course, would have been, if the High Authority had never allowed any exemption from the surcharges and strictly based its program on the consumption of scrap metal. For the concerns whose profit picture was likely to be darkened by the High Authority's concept of what constituted "own" scrap, the best course of action would have been a rapid change in their legal structure. This was done by Mannesmann at the end of 1958 when it combined all subsidiaries into one legal personality, but unfortunately it was too late to reap substantial advantages from this change in the scrap subsidy scheme.

Although the scrap metal equalization system is now a thing of the past, the litigations that have arisen from the problems in connection with this system clearly illustrate the great power of the Court in the economic field. And the end of the litigations in this area is not yet in sight. The final bills for the surcharge payments presented by the High Authority are disputed by a number of steel producers for a variety of reasons. As of June 17, 1963, forty-seven actions were pending before the Court which were brought by steel producers against the High Authority in connection with these disputes.[1]

Another difficult problem under the ECSC Treaty has been the application of the Treaty's anti-trust regulations to the German coal sales organization in the Ruhr. The basic causes for this difficulty have been two-fold. First, the distribution of coal in the major coal producing countries of Western Europe has been traditionally in the hands of strong cartels. Second, at the time that the Treaty was concluded and during the early years of its existence there was a shortage of coal. In 1958, however, conditions changed; the ascendancy of other fuels and unfavorable market conditions in general resulted in considerable over-production of coal and the situation has not improved much even today.

In France the coal mines are nationalized and imports of coal are handled by a semi-official organization, the *Association Technique de l'Importation Charbonnière* (A.T.I.C.), which serves as a protective screen for the French coal mining industry. In 1958 the High Authority asserted that the activities of A.T.I.C. were violating the fair competition principles of the ECSC Treaty and brought suit against that organization. However, the dispute was settled out of Court when A.T.I.C. agreed to modify its method of operations.[2] In Belgium, beset by problems of inef-

[1] *List of Cases Pending Before the Court*, June 17, 1963.
[2] Louis Lister, *Europe's Coal and Steel Community* (New York, 1960) pp. 269, 270, and Case No. 7/58.

ficient coal mines which had to be closed, one sales organization *(Comptoir Belge des Charbons)* distributes about 77% of the coal production, but its members retain their independence with respect to price formation of the various categories of coal.[1] In the matter of German coal, however, a running battle has been fought since 1953 between the sales organizations for Ruhr coal and the High Authority which continues today and during which the Court has rendered several important decisions.[2] It should be noted that coal mined in the Ruhr region makes up nearly 50% of all coal consumed in the Member States and represents more than 90% of all coal produced in Germany.

A few days before the ECSC Treaty went into effect, the German Ruhr coal producers placed under the control of one organization the sales for all Ruhr coal mines, privately or state owned, despite the fact that the anti-trust regulations for the Treaty were well known. The High Authority invoking the Convention containing the Transitional Provisions gave provisional authorization to this single sales organization pending a study of this matter. Finally, in 1956, the High Authority ordered a reorganization of the single sales agency into three companies to be called "Geitling," "Mausegatt," and "President." This was considered to be an adequate solution to meet the requirements of the anti-trust provisions of the Treaty although the three new agencies were of equal structure and operated from the same locality and all exports continued to be handled by a single sales agency. Dissatisfied with the manner in which the three sales agencies operated, the High Authority ordered in 1959 additional changes in their organization in order to ensure some measure of competition.[3] The coal producers appealed to the Court, which, however, sustained in general the orders of the High Authority. Despite the

---

[1] Parlement Européen, *Rapport sur le onzième rapport general sur l'activité de la Communauté européenne du charbon et de l'acier,* June 18, 1963, pp. 4, 5.

[2] For instance, Ruhrkohlen-Verkaufsgesellschaften "Geitling," "Mausegatt" and "President" v. High Authority, Dec. Nos. 16–18/59, February 12, 1960, 6/I Rec. 45 (1960) and Ruhrkolhen-Verkaufsgesellschaften "Geitling," "Mausegatt" and "President" supported by the government of the State Nordrhein-Westfalen v. High Authority, Dec. No. 13/60, May 18, 1962, 8 Rec. 165 (1962).

[3] For details see Lister, *op.cit.,* pp. 259–267.

Court's decision, the coal producers submitted in 1960 to the High Authority a proposal under which they asked permission to have at least a part of their production sold by one single sales organization. The High Authority denied this permission whereupon the coal producers again appealed the decision of the High Authority to the Court. In the very detailed and thorough judgment of May 18, 1962, the Court held that the single sales organization proposed by the Ruhr coal producers did not meet the requirements of the Treaty and that a minimum degree of competition as required by the Treaty would be guaranteed only by the continued existence and functioning of three separate sales agencies.

Although the Court in its judgment leaned over backward to take into consideration realistically the market conditions existing in the coal industry and emphasized the minimum requirements it had postulated for meeting the demands of the Treaty, the High Authority issued in March of 1963 a new decision on the matter in which it acceded to a request of the German coal producers to reduce the number of sales agencies from three to two organizations of equal structure.[1] The chief of the anti-trust division of the High Authority attempted to save the day by advocating that the two proposed sales agencies should at least be structured differently. In particular, he recommended that all state-owned coal mines should be assigned to one of the two agencies instead of being equally divided between the two organizations. Although he was supported by the Belgian and Dutch members of the High Authority, his recommendations were not accepted.[2] There were, however, some improvements which should be noted although they may not have been very significant.

---

[1] Dec. No. 5/63 and 6/63 of March 20, 1963, *Journal Officiel* (April 10, 1963), pp. 1173 to 1209/63. In this connection see also the critical comments regarding the judgment of the Court of May 18, 1962 (detailed identification on p. 77, footnote 2 *supra*.) made by Maurice Bye," L'Arrêt 13–30 du 18 mai 1962 sur les comptoirs de la Ruhr," *Droit Social* (May 1963), pp. 257–272.

[2] This information was related to the writer by Mr. Johannes Petrick, the chief of the anti-trust division of the High Authotity. According to Mr. Petrick the Ruhr coal producers and officials of the German government exerted strong pressures on the supposedly independent members of the High Authority to accept the proposed new system for the sale of Ruhr coal.

The two new sales agencies do not occupy common offices as did the former three agencies. Their bookkeeping systems are now almost completely independent, and exports are now handled separately by each agency instead of being conducted by one common organization. Nevertheless, these improvements did not deter the government of the Netherlands from lodging an appeal against the authorization of the two Ruhr coal sales agencies by the High Authority and this appeal is now pending before the Court, but most likely will not be decided until the middle of 1964.[1]

The problems of the Ruhr coal sales organization for which the Court has been asked to find solutions, require really much more than a judicial interpretation and application of the Treaty. These problems demand an economic and political solution which might involve a change of the Treaty. A "small" revision of the Treaty aiming at a liberalization of its anti-trust regulations to meet the changed market conditions in the coal industry was attempted by the High Authority and the Council in 1961, but failed to obtain the approval of the Court which considered the proposed revision too broad.[2] As a consequence, it might be necessary to amend the Treaty by agreement of the Member States in order to adapt its provisions to the prevailing economic and political realities which obviously do not support a vigorous competition among sellers of coal, since it seems to place into jeopardy the large investments of the coal industry and the jobs of many miners.[3] The alternative would be that the anti-trust provisions of the Treaty would be reduced to a sham and a farce, a development which would greatly disparage the respect for the "rule of law" within the Communities and thus diminish the prospects for a united Europe. In this connection some observations made in the Report of the European Parliament on the

---

[1] Case No. 66/63 of March 20, 1963.

[2] See pp. 62–63 *supra*.

[3] The European Parliament would like to see another effort made by the High Authority and the Council of Ministers to carry through a small revision of the Treaty to "adapt" several provisions of the Treaty to the new conditions. (See p. 37 of the report cited on p. 77, footnote 1 *supra*.

Activity of the High Authority in 1962 appear to be quite significant:

The political influence of the High Authority within the European community was-especially in recent times – less noticeable than could be anticipated.
There are several reasons for this unusual situation. Problems, with which the High Authority was confronted and of which some were of decisive significance, such as the structural coal crisis, had not been foreseen by the framers of the Treaty. Therefore, possibilities for a solution [of these problems,] in part, did not lie anymore within the framework of the Treaty.... As a consequence, the powers of the High Authority for decisions or for recommendations could not be exercised to their full extent and it was necessary to fall back on the classic method of international collaboration, which is characterized by the need for unanimous decisions.
From the frequent consultations with the governments of the Member States the High Authority apparently has developed the inclination to consult these governments before working out a solution of problems even in those cases in which it is *not* by law obligated to do so.... Herein lies a serious danger, not only for the position of the High Authority itself, but generally for the European Community of Coal and Steel and for the entire European integration.[1]

D. THE CIVIL JURISDICTION OF THE COURT

The Court's civil jurisdiction falls into several categories. First, the Court is competent for disputes between the Communities' civil servants and the institutions that employ them. Although in several European states such disputes are decided by administrative courts, in the common law sense the Court exercises "civil" jurisdiction in such cases.[2] Second, the Court has jurisdiction over suits for damages brought against the Communities or against individual civil servants in cases of tort. Third, the Court's civil jurisdiction might be stipulated in a contract, under public or private law, to which one of the Communities is a party or which is concluded in its behalf.[3]

---

[1] *Ibid.*, p. 36.
[2] See also Bächle, *op.cit.*, p. 23, and Wohlfarth *et al.*, *op.cit.*, comments 3e before Article 164.
[3] Articles 40, 42 ECSC Treaty, 178, 179, 181, 215 EEC Treaty and 151, 152, 153 and 188 Euratom Treaty.

Civil Service Matters

While the Rome Treaties specifically stipulate the competence of the Court in any case between the Communities and their employees, the ECSC Treaty does not contain a similar provision. However, the competence of the Court is now clearly established in the personnel statutes for the civil servants of all three Communities.[1]

In litigations between the Communities and their civil servants involving pecuniary interests and in other cases specified by the personnel statutes of the Communities the Court has full review powers. This means that it can review the manner in which discretionary authority has been used by an agency of the Communities in arriving at a decision which has caused a grievance, and that it can set aside or alter such a decision. In this connection the opinions of the Court expressed in the judgments in two civil service cases rendered in 1956 are significant inasmuch as they reflect the concept of the Court with regard to the limits of its review power under the personnel statutes. The Court disclaimed any proficiency for evaluating purely administrative factors, for which only an administrative agency possessed specialized knowledge. However, it deemed itself authorized to examine the methods employed for reaching a decision and to investigate whether the discretion underlying the decision was exercised "conscientiously" or whether the decision was based upon an abuse of discretionary powers.[2] Thus, the Court has the power of not only checking into the observance of statutory limits and legal procedures, but apparently also in the motives and purposes of the decision. In addition, it seems that the Court has the power to determine whether the findings made and the conclusions reached by the administrative agency in the exercise of its discretionary authority are supported by substantial evidence, but not whether the facts justify the decision. It appears, there-

---

[1] Article 91 of the Personnel Statutes. For the complete text see *Journal Officiel*, June 14, 1962, pp. 1385/62–1460/62.

[2] Miranda Mirrosevich v. High Authority, Dec. No. 10/55, December 12, 1956, 2 Rec. 365 (1955/56) and René Bourgaux v. Common Assembly, Dec. No. 1/56, December 17, 1956, 3 Rec. 421 (1955–56).

fore, that "full" review of discretionary authority of an administrative agency grants the Court powers to examine both law and fact with few limitations, powers considerably broader than those possessed by American courts.[1]

Of the 113 judgments and opinions rendered by the Court from 1953 until July 31, 1963, fifteen decisions pertained to cases brought by civil servants against the Communities. Nine of these decisions were either wholly or partially in favor of the complainants. In several of these judgments one appears to sense an effort by the Court to extend its protective hand over the fledgling civil service of the Communities.[2] In some decisions the Court recognized the existence of subjective rights of the civil servants which can not be rescinded retroactively nor without indemnification.[3] In another decision, the Court awarded each plaintiff 60,000 Belgian franks *"ex aequo et bono"* although the plaintiffs had either been reinstated or found other employment. The Court wanted to compensate them for "the worry caused by the hazardous situation created by the default of the Commission." [4] In one case, the Court overruled its own president who as chief executive of the Court had issued an order cancelling an allowance of one of his civil servants; the justices declared the order null and void because according to their opinion it was based on an erroneous interpretation of the personnel statutes.[5]

During the last several months, many of the temporary employees of the Communities have been integrated as permanent officials of the Communities. This process of integration which is continuing has brought a number of complaints to the Court from those who were not integrated. By the end of February, 1964,

---

[1] "Full review" must be understood in the same or similiar sense as the French law term of *"Recours de pleine juridiction"* that is used in the French text of the Treaty. For fuller information on this subject see Schwartz, *op.cit.*, pp. 192–242.

[2] Cf. Feld, "Civil Service" for details on these cases.

[3] For instance Dineke Algera *et al.* v. Common Assembly, Dec. Nos. 7/56 and 3-7/57, July 12, 1957, 3 Rec. 81 (1957).

[4] Eva von Lachmüller *et al.* v. EEC Commission, Dec. Nos. 43/59, 45/59, and 48/59, July 15, 1960, 6/I Rec. 933, (1960).

[5] Gabriel Simon v. Court of Justice of the European Communities, Dec. No. 15/60, June 1, 1960, 7 Rec. 223 (1961).

already 28 cases were pending in which disappointed temporary civil servants had filed suits against their institutions for refusal of integration. The Court anticipates many more suits to be filed in this matter in the months to come.

Liability of the Communities

Under all three Treaties the Court has jurisdiction in cases arising from any contractual liability of the Communities only if such competence is stipulated in a contract to which one of the Communities is a party.[1] With regard to non-contractual or tortious liability of the Communities, the ECSC Treaty and the Rome Treaties are at variance.

Under the ECSC Treaty the Court is competent to decide about actions for damages brought by enterprises which have sustained a "direct and special injury" through an act of the High Authority that has been annulled by the Court and adjudged as "involving a fault for which the Community is liable." In such a case the High Authority must make equitable reparation, and if such proves to be impossible, it must grant reasonable damages.[2] In addition, the Court has jurisdiction over cases in which compensation is demanded by any party who has sustained injury from an "official fault" of a Community organ in the execution of the Treaty. In the event that such an injury results from a "personal fault" of a civil servant in the performance of his duties, the Court may assess damages against him. However, should the injured party be unable to recover damages from the civil servant, the Court is authorized to assess equitable damages against the Community.[3]

The distinction between "official fault" and "personal fault" is used in French administrative law and requires an explanation.

---

[1] Articles 42, ECSC Treaty, 181 EEC Treaty and 153 Euratom Treaty.

[2] Article 34.

[3] Article 40 (1 and 2). See also article 47 which specifically states that "any violation by the High Authority of trade secrecy which has caused damage to an enterprise may be the subject of a suit for damages before the Court..." Cf. also S. A. Antoine Vloeberghs A.G. v. High Authority, Dec. Nos. 9 and 12/60, July 14, 1961, 7 Rec. 391 (1961) at pp. 424–427.

Official faults are those that arise out of an inherent deficiency of the administrative machinery, regardless of any culpable action on the part of a particular individual, whereas a personal fault implies a wrong committed by a particular individual for which he is censurable.[1] In other words, for an individual to have committed a personal fault, must have involved at least negligence on the part of the individual.

The Rome Treaties do not differentiate between "official" and "personal" fault. They stipulate quite generally that "as regards non-contractual liability, the Community shall, in accordance with the general principles common to the laws of Member States, make reparation for any damage caused by its institutions or by its employees in the performance of their duties." [2] In all such cases, the Court of the Communities has exclusive jurisdiction.[3] These provisions impose upon the Court a challenging as well as very difficult task. It must utilize the art of comparative law – a sub-discipline, which is being studied more and more in the law schools of the world – to develop a uniform new law. So far, the Court has not had occasion to apply these provisions although it has drawn on the legal systems of the Member States extensively when bridging gaps in the Treaties.[4]

In the event that damages have been assessed against one of the three Communities, and these damages were the consequence of a "serious fault" on the part of a civil servant in the exercise of his office or incident to the exercise of his official functions, the Communities can require the civil servant to compensate them for the loss.[5] The term "serious fault" seems to indicate that a liability of the civil servant toward the Communities exists only when a wrongful act is motivated by willful intent or malice or is the result of gross negligence. The Court of Justice is competent to decide cases relating to compensation

---

[1] Valentine, *op.cit.*, pp. 113, 114. The French terms are *faute de service* and *faute personelle.*
[2] Articles 215 EEC Treaty and 188 Euratom Treaty.
[3] Articles 178 EEC Treaty and 151 Euratom Treaty.
[4] See pp. 88–89 *infra.*
[5] Article 22 of the Personnel Statutes.

for damage instituted by the Communities against their civil servants. In such cases the Court has the power of "full review" [1] and is authorized to set aside and change the decisions of the Communities' institutions.

E. MISCELLANEOUS COMPETENCES OF THE COURT

As has been stated in the introduction to this chapter, the four broad categories used for the classification of the Court's jurisdiction do not exhaust the list of the competences which the Court possesses or which can be assigned to it by the organs of the Communities or private parties. Some of the additional jurisdictional powers – those which might assume a measure of significance in the future – will now be briefly discussed in this section.

In certain instances the Court may act as a disciplinary tribunal. In this capacity, the Court participates in the removal of a member of the High Authority or the Commissions in the event that such an individual should no longer fulfill the conditions required for the performance of his duties or should have committed a serious offence. In such a case the Court may be petitioned by the Council of Ministers or by the other members of the High Authority or the Commissions to declare their colleague removed from office. [2]

With regard to the European Investment Bank, an institution established under the EEC Treaty, the Court has been given certain, specific jurisdictional powers. It is competent to hear cases concerning the fulfillment of the obligations of the Member States arising under the Statute of the European Investment Bank, regarding the conclusions of the Board of Governors of the Bank if an appeal is lodged by a Member State or the Commission, and regarding the conclusions of the Board of Directors of the Bank in the event of similar appeals. [3]

Under the Euratom Treaty the Court has jurisdiction, including the power of "full review," in cases involving the grant

[1] Article 22(3) of the Personnel Statutes. For the term "full review" cf. pp. 81' 82 *supra*.
[2] Articles 12(2) ECSC Treaty, 160 EEC Treaty, and 129 Euratom Treaty.
[3] Article 180 EEC Treaty.

by the Commission of licences of patents owned by the Community and regarding appeals brought by individuals and enterprises against the imposition of penalties by the Commission. Furthermore, if the Commission considers that a person or enterprise has committed an infringement of the Treaty and if a Member State does not impose any penalties in such a matter in accordance with its municipal law after having been invited to do so by the Commission, the latter may refer the matter to the Court.[1]

The ECSC grants the Court also jurisdiction in cases in which an enterprise appeals the imposition of penalty payments or of pecuniary sanctions by the High Authority. Again, as under the Euratom Treaty in similar cases, the Court is authorized to "fully" review the decisions of the High Authority.[2] The EEC Treaty does not contain similar specific provisions as do the ECSC and Euratom Treaties. However, it grants the Council of Ministers a general authorization to provide for penalties in the quasi-legislative regulations it issues and to bestow upon the Court jurisdiction in disputes regarding the enforcement of such penalties. Such jurisdiction includes the power of "full review" and of reversing and altering decisions of the organs of the Community. All regulations issued by the Council in force at present contain enforceable penalties and give the Court full jurisdiction to review these penalties.[3]

Finally, the Treaties permit the Member States to assign to the Court, under the terms of a *compromis*, the function of arbitrating a dispute between them, provided that the dispute is connected with the object of one of the Treaties.[4] An assignment of arbitration functions to the Court, however, is not admissible for those subject matters for which the jurisdiction of the Court has already been specified by the Treaties.[5]

---

[1] Articles 144, 145, 12 and 83 of the Euratom Treaty. See also Daig, *op.cit.*, pp. 185–189, 193, 194 for more details on these competences.

[2] Article 36(2). See also Valentine, *op.cit.*, pp. 99 and 100.

[3] Article 172. See also Alan Campbell and Dennis Thompson, *Common Market Law* (London, 1962), comments to article 172.

[4] Articles 89(2) ECSC Treaty, 182 EEC Treaty, and 154 Euratom Treaty.

[5] See Wohlfarth *et al.*, *op.cit.*, comment 1 to article 182 and cf. articles 89 (1) ECSC Treaty, 170 EEC Treaty, and 142 Euratom Treaty. See also p. 37, *supra*.

CHAPTER IV

SOURCES OF LAW

The Statute of the International Court of Justice at The Hague
specifies the sources of law which should guide the Court in
deciding a case. According to that Statute the Court shall apply
international conventions, international custom, the general
principles of law recognized by civilized nations, and "judicial
decisions and the teachings of the most highly qualified publicists." [1] In contrast, none of the Community Treaties refers to
the sources of law which the Court of the Communities must
apply when interpreting each Treaty. Each of the Treaties merely
states, as has been quoted earlier, that "The Court of Justice shall
ensure observance of law and justice in the interpretation and
application of this Treaty." [2]

The assumption is justified that the omission of an article
specifying the sources of law for the Court was not due merely to
negligence. Rather, the Communities were such an unprece-
dented and complex legal experiment that at the time of the
drafting of the Treaties it was almost impossible to envisage in
detail the various legal relationships and the proper sources of
law governing them. As the practice of the Court over the years
reveals, there is no danger that it ever was or will be at a loss for
a "source of law"; the richness and diversity of the sources it has
drawn upon are remarkable. [3]

---

[1] Article 38.

[2] Articles 164 EEC Treaty and 136 Euratom Treaty. The French and German
texts use only the words "observation of law"; the words "and justice" in the English
translation appear to be surplus to the translation. See Campbell and Thompson,
op.cit., p. 92 and comments to article 164. In article 31 of the ECSC Treaty the
following words are added: "and of the regulations for its execution," but the term
"and justice" does not appear in the English text.

[3] McMahon, *op.cit.*, p. 327 and Bebr, *Judicial Control, op.cit.*, p. 26. For a detailed

The most important source of the Community law is, of course, found in the Treaties, to which several protocols, lists, and supplementary conventions are annexed. It is the standard by which all activities of the institutions of the Communities are tested.

A second important source of Community law is Found in the regulations and other acts of the institutions of the Communities, particularly the Council of Ministers, the High Authority, and the Commissions. The "law-making" process in the Communities is based upon the more or less specific authorizations in the Treaties. Beyond that, however, gaps in the legal framework of the Common Market and Euratom may be filled by the utilization of a "general clause" contained in the Rome Treaties. This clause authorizes the Council to enact appropriate provisions in cases where the Treaties have not provided for the requisite powers of action.[1] In the ECSC Treaty the "small revision" of the Treaty is available for the same purpose. This procedure, however, is rather restricted in its application, as has been shown earlier.[2] Finally, the practices of the institutions of the Communities may lay a basis for the development of customary rules that could constitute a source of law for the Court.

Thirdly, the municipal laws, municipal decisions (especially the decisions of the *Conseil d'Etat*, the French Administrative High Court), and the writings of important legal publicists in the Member States form a fertile and very vital source of law for the Court.[3] As has been already seen, the EEC and Euratom refer explicitly to the "general principles common to the laws of the Member States" as the source of law to govern tort cases under

discussion of the Court's sources of law under the ECSC Treaty see Pierre Mathijsen, *Le droit de la Communauté Européenne du Charbon et de l'Acier, Une étude des sources* (The Hague, 1958).

[1] Articles 235 EEC Treaty and 203 Euratom Treaty. The Council must act by means of unanimous vote after having received a proposal from the Commission and after the Parliament has been consulted. See also p. 43 and its, footnote 1, *supra*.

[2] See the discussion of Article 95 of the ECSC Treaty on pp. 60–63 *supra*.

[3] See the conclusions of Advocate-General Lagrange in De Gezamenlijke Steenkolenmijnen in Limburg v. High Authority, Dec. No. 17/57, February 4, 1959, 5 Rec. 9 (1958/59) at p. 36.

these Treaties.[1] The Court is here clearly required to scrutinize the six national legal systems for common principles and develop from this the law for the Communities. Such a process has also been applied by the Court in disputes that have arisen under the ECSC Treaty. In his conclusions presented in a case in 1954, Advocate-General Lagrange stated that the study of the national legal systems must be undertaken each time when it is necessary to arrive at an elaboration of what the law of the Treaty is.[2] The Court itself stated in a later case that in the event that it could not find a rule in the Treaty itself, it was compelled to take into account "the rules recognized in the legislation, doctrine and jurisprudence of the Member State." [3] However, even where the Treaties have adopted a concept from a particular national system, such as the French notion of *détournement de pouvoir*, the Court has sought to devise a definition of its own and applicable only within the Community law rather than taking over the meaning of the term uniquely from the French law.[4]

Professor Bebr points out that the general references of the Treaties to municipal laws are mere sign posts for the general direction along which the Court may develop the Community law. He warns the Court to avoid a servile imitation of municipal laws and of the jurisprudence of national courts. Rather, the Court must creatively form a synthesis out of municipal laws and bring them into accord with the objectives and needs of the Communities and their political and economic climate. The Court's creative function is particularly crucial when the municipal laws are contradictory. As in such an event there is no common, underlying principle, the Court must evaluate and weigh the differences, reconcile them, and shape them in accordance with the purposes of the Communities.[5]

---

[1] Articles 215 EEC Treaty and 188 Euratom Treaty.

[2] Associazione Industrie Siderurgiche Italiane v. High Authority, Dec. No. 3/54, February 10, 1955, 1 Rec. 123 (1954–55) at p. 148.

[3] Dincke Algera *et al.* v. Common Assembly, Dec. Nos. 7/56 and 3 to 7/57, 3 Rec. 81 (1951) at p. 115.

[4] See p. 68 *supra*.

[5] Bebr. *Judicial Control, op.cit.*, pp. 28, 29.

The role of international law as a source of law for the Court has so far been only minor. A reason for this may be found in a statement by Mr. Lagrange in 1955 that

> our Court is not an international tribunal, but is concerned with the jurisdiction within a community which has been created by six states and which resembles more a federation than an international organization.... [T]he Treaty... although concluded in the form of international treaties and undoubtedly being one, nevertheless also constitutes from a substantive point of view the charter of the Community and as a consequence the legal provisions derived from the Treaty must be viewed as the internal law of the Community. As for the sources of this law, nothing prevents that in a given case they may be sought in international law, however normally, and most frequently, they are found in the municipal law of the Member States.[1]

There may, of course, be occasions when international law in the form of international agreements may provide a source of Community law. An example would be an agreement concluded by one of the Communities as a person under international law with third states such as a trade agreement, or an agreement among Member States that may pertain to the harmonization of corporation law or the elimination of double-taxation.[2] In addition, the EEC Treaty provisions governing the association of overseas territories with the Community specify that such association must be accomplished in conformity with the principles stated in the preamble to the Treaty. Since this preamble refers to the Charter of the United Nations, it may be assumed that an agreement of association must take into consideration the principles of the Charter such as the principle of self-determination.[3] Finally, the EEC and Euratom Treaties specify that the contractual liability of the two Communities shall be governed by the law applying to the contract concerned. In respect to contracts made to which the Community is a party, the rules of international private law will apply.[4]

As a last source of law must be considered the Court's own

[1] Fédération Charbonnière de Belgique v. High Authority, Dec. No. 8/55, July 16, 1956, 2 Rec. 151 (1955/56) at p. 263.
[2] See article 220 EEC Treaty.
[3] See article 131(3) of the EEC Treaty and Stein and Hay, *op.cit.*, p. 505.
[4] Articles 215(1) EEC Treaty and 188 Euratom Treaty.

jurisprudence. This source of law is particularly important in cases where the Court interprets incomplete or ambiguous provisions of the Treaty. Although Continental legal theory is generally opposed to judge-made law and although the Treaties do not contain a rule or law of precedent, an interpretation of the Treaty once adopted is likely to be followed in future cases. Thus, the Court in effect makes law and this assumption is strengthened by the fact that there is no resort to a higher judicial institution nor is there a parliament endowed with broad legislative powers. The only means of overruling a decision by the Court is either by a judgment of the Court itself or through the cumbersome amendment process of the Treaties requiring the ratification by all Member States.

While so far the discussion has primarily dealt with the sources of law which the Court applies, a few comments are in order as to the methods of interpretation the Court utilizes. In the judgments of the Court one rarely finds any theoretical discussion concerning the principles of interpretation to be applied. Obviously, the Court wishes to avoid taking any doctrinal position which might severely limit its freedom of action in the future. From the practice of the Court, however, it is possible to draw certain conclusions as to its techniques of interpretation.

The Court will not interpret a text which is quite clear. This, of course, is in accordance with the usual principles of interpretation. Otherwise, however, the Court seems to favor, more often than not, a flexible and dynamic approach to the interpretation of ambiguous or unclear phrases.

Some clarification of such phrases may be gained by comparing the French, German, Italian, and Dutch versions of the EEC and Euratom Treaties since all four versions are equally authentic. The purpose of this comparison, which at times tends to deepen the confusion rather than clarify it, is to find the true scope of the provision and to select the version which best serves the purposes of the Treaty.[1] Since the ECSC Treaty only recognizes the French

[1] Cf. Daig, *op.cit.*, p. 157.

text as authentic,[1] a comparison of versions for the sake of clarifying doubtful phrases of that Treaty is not useful.

While comparatively few preparatory materials of the Treaties are available to serve as an aid to establishing the intent of the framers, records of the ratification debates, although of much more limited value, are at hand in adequate numbers. The Court has acknowledged the validity of these documents for the interpretation of the Treaties but has warned that they must be used with prudence and must not be allowed to contradict the text.[2] On the other hand, since many legal concepts embodied in the Treaties, are borrowed from the municipal law of the Member States, the Court frequently analyzes and synthesizes the municipal laws of the different Member States in order to arrive at the meaning of an ambivalent provision. The Court stated in a rather early decision that it was necessary "to call upon the law of the different Member States in order to arrive at a meaningful interpretation of our Community law."[3] It should not be thought, however, that the Court always refers to the law of all the Member States. If it regards a particular concept as peculiar to one or two countries, then it will only examine the jurisprudence of those two countries.[4] Sometimes, it will only refer to French law and no other.[5] Occasionally, one finds the Court referring to "general principles of law, applicable even without text" stating that it is necessary to include "the general principles of law in the rules for the application of the Treaty" without making clear to which general principles it is referring.[6]

It has already been mentioned earlier that in its jurisprudence

[1] Article 100.
[2] Gabriel Simon v. Court of Justice of the European Communities, Dec. No. 5/60, June 1, 1961, 7 Rec. 223 (1961) at pp. 244 and 256.
[3] Conclusions of Advocate-General Roemer in Government of the Kingdom of the Netherlands v. High Authority, Dec. No. 6/54, March 18, 1955, I Rec. 201 (1954/55) at p. 232.
[4] Conclusions of Advocate-General Lagrange in Associazione Industrie Siderurgiche Italiane v. High Authority, Dec. No. 5/55, June 28, 1955, 1 Rec. 263 (1954–55) at p. 288.
[5] Conclusions of Advocate-General Roemer in Groupements des Industries Sidérurgiques Luxembourgoises v. High Authority, Dec. Nos. 7 and 9/54, April 23, 1956, 2 Rec. 53 (1955/56) at p. 120.
[6] Conclusions of Advocate-General Lagrange in Barbara Erzbergbau *et al.* v. High

the Court has placed particular emphasis on the basic principles and objectives of the Treaties.[1] With regard to the interpretation of the Treaties, Advocate-General Lagrange stated in his conclusions in one of the early cases decided by the Court that

...in the interpretation of the ECSC Treaty, it would be dangerous to hold only to the letter of the text. In order to discover the economic objectives assigned to a particular provision, one must consider the fundamental objectives and principles of the Treaty.[2]

Such teleological interpretation is particularly well suited to the needs of an international organization because it provides an excellent tool for filling the gaps that are often found in the texts of the underlying treaties. In its more recent jurisprudence, the Court, after interpreting an ambiguous provision, has added "that this reasoning is confirmed by the Treaties instituting the European Economie Community and the Coal and Steel Community,"[3] thus invoking the totality of the Community law in support of its interpretation.

When interpreting international agreements and when defining the relations of the Community with third countries, the Court will most likely also resort to the rules of interpretation customary in international law which tend to be relatively restrictive. So far the Court has not consciously applied these rules although in one instance the Court applied a rule of interpretation which it considered as "generally recognized both in international and national law."[4]

Authority, Dec. Nos. 3–18/58, 25 and 26/58, May 10, 1960, 6/I Rec. 367 (1960) at p. 427 and Felten and Guillaume *et al.* v. High Authority, Dec. No. 21/58, July 6, 1959, 5 Rec. 211 (1958/59) at p. 221.

[1] See p. 39, *supra*.

[2] Royal Government of the Netherlands v. High Authority, Dec. No. 6/54, March 21, 1955, 1 Rec. 201 (1954–55) at p. 232.

[3] For example Jean E. Humblet v. the Belgian State, Dec. No. 6/60, December 16, 1960, 6/II Rec. 1125 (1960) at pp. 1154 and 1156.

[4] Fédération Charbonnière de Belgique v. High Authority, Dec. No. 8/55, November 29, 1956, 2 Rec. 291 (1955/56) at p. 305. Of interest in this respect is also a statement of Advocate-General Lagrange in his conclusions to an earlier judgment of the Court in the same matter (June 12, 1956, 2 Rec. 201, at pp. 263, 264) in which he declared that he could not actually find two different doctrines for the interpretation of internal and international law, but that in practice the international courts tended to be more reluctant "to deviate from the literal application of a provision than the national courts...."

CHAPTER V

PROCEDURE

A case is initiated before the Court of Justice by addressing a petition to the registrar. This petition must contain the necessary identifying data, the subject-matter of the dispute, a short summary of the grounds on which the petition is based, and supporting evidence. Upon receipt of the petition, the president of the Court assigns the case to one of the two chambers for the task of hearing evidence and appoints a *juge rapporteur* from among the judges of that chamber. The "reporting judge" has the task of making a preliminary investigation of the case and of preparing a preliminary report for the chamber's president.[1]

In the proceedings before the Court private parties such as individuals or enterprises must be represented by counsel who may be either a member of the bar of one of the Member States or a professor of law who according to his national law is allowed to practice before domestic courts. The Member States and the institutions of the Communities are not required to make use of counsel, but their representatives may be assisted by an advocate who must have the same qualifications as counsel for private parties.[2]

The Written and Oral Phases of the Proceedings

The procedure before the Court is divided into a written and an oral stage. During the written stage normally four briefs are exchanged between the contending parties. The petition of the

[1] Articles 19 of the Statute of the Court (EEC), 18, Euratom Statute, 22, ECSC Statute and 24 (2) of the Rules of Procedure. (Hereinafter, only the article numbers of the EEC Statute are cited unless there should be substantive differences between the three statutes.)

[2] Articles 17 of the Statute; see also articles 32–36 of the Rules of Procedure.

complainant mentioned above is answered by the defendant and this exchange is followed by a rejoinder of the complainant to which the defendant may submit another reply.[1] These briefs, containing not only pleadings, but also extensive legal arguments, documentary evidence, and supporting papers, are quite bulky and their exchange normally takes several months. The institutions of the Communities whose decisions are in dispute receive copies of the briefs as well as of all documentary evidence and supporting papers.

During the preliminary investigation the Court may request the parties to produce all documents and to supply all information which the Court considers desirable. If necessary, the personal appearance of the parties may be ordered. In addition, the Court may also request Member States and institutions not being parties to the case to supply all information which the Court deems essential for the proceedings. During this phase of the proceedings witnesses are also called by the parties and by the Court; in addition the Court may request studies and testimony by experts.[2]

Witnesses and experts may be sworn in accordance with the laws of their national states. If any violation of their oath is committed and if the Court of Justice reports such a violation, the Member States are obliged to regard this in the same manner as a breach of law before a domestic court and must prosecute the violator. In accordance with this mission of assisting the Court in rendering a just decision, the advocate-general can also request the hearing of witnesses and may question them during the taking of evidence. A public record is made by the registrar of the proceedings of the hearings of witnesses and experts.[3]

Oral hearings are scheduled only after all relevant information has been collected, testimony heard, and expert reports received in the preliminary investigation. During the oral procedure the report of the *juge-rapporteur* is presented to the Court sitting in

[1] Articles 37–42 of the Rules of Procedure.
[2] Articles 21 and 22 of the Statute and 47 and 49 of the Rules of Procedure.
[3] Article 25, 27 of the Statute and 47(4) and 53 of the Rules of Procedure.

plenary session which then proceeds to hear the final oral arguments of counsel of the parties. The judges of the Court as well as the advocates-general may direct questions at counsel and the Court may order the taking of additional evidence either by the chamber or by the *juge-rapporteur* if this is deemed necessary. Finally, the advocate-general presents his conclusions and observations to the Court. Both the preliminary investigation and the oral hearings are public unless otherwise ordered by the Court.[1]

The written and oral phases of the procedure before the Court have recently been the subject of some severe criticism. Professor Conrad Zweigert of the University of Hamburg has asserted that the Court has emphasized too much the written phase of the procedure and that the oral phase has become "more or less a mere facade." [2] The Court has been characterized as a "silent tribunal" inasmuch as "the pleading party learns only from the judgment whether it has been lucky enough to present arguments with regard to the legal questions which the Court considered as important." With the exception of occasional queries, the Court is said to be silent as to the importance it attaches to the various legal questions. Thus, counsel might deal only briefly with the question of the admissibility of the suit but might argue at length with regard to the substantive issues of the case, whereas the Court all along had deemed the problem of admissibility as the most important issue of the case. As a consequence, it has been suggested that the oral hearings should be preceeded by consultations between the Court and counsel of the contending parties during which the Court should identify the issues it considered as significant and divulge the questions about which it was doubtful and desired additional information. In this way, the oral hearings would be conducted in a more efficient manner and would be more meaningful for the Court as well as for the parties concerned.[3] At the same time, a situation might be

---

[1] Articles 54–60 and 46(2) of the Rules of Procedure.

[2] Zweigert, *op.cit.*

[3] It is interesting to note that at least one of the judges has complained that the presentations of arguments by counsel in the oral sessions were too long. Judge Riese, *op.cit.*, p. 272, considered such presentations lasting 24 hours in one case and more

avoided in which the Court may become fully conscious of the legal significance of certain points in a dispute only after the oral hearings had been completed, but might nevertheless proceed to render a judgment without further hearing the parties because a re-entry into oral proceedings is rejected as being too cumbersome.

Professor Zweigert has also criticized the methods which the Court has been using for the presentation of evidence and has suggested certain changes of the Rules of Procedure in order to improve the determination of relevant facts in cases before the Court. Although Advocate-General Lagrange has defended the existing procedures of the Court against Professor Zweigert's criticism and has opposed his suggested innovations, other members of the Court seem to feel that Professor Zweigert's arguments were not without merit.[1] Obviously the procedure of any newly established court requires an extensive period of trial and error before a satisfactory practice can be developed.

The Language Problem

A difficult problem in the procedure before the Court is presented by the recognition of four official languages: French, German, Italian, and Dutch. The Rules of Procedure of the Court establish the basic principle that the plaintiff may select the language in which the case will be heard, but there are important exceptions to this rule. If the defendant is the government of a Member State or a natural or legal person residing in a Member State, the case is heard in the language of the defendant. Since the judges have not been chosen for their linguistic ability, but for their knowledge of the law, all documents brought before the Court are translated in each of the three other languages and during the oral procedure a simultaneous translation is provided. Furthermore, all publications of the Court such as judgments are

than 60 hours in another as excessive, particularly since the conclusions of the advocate-general frequently also fill the whole day.

[1] This impression was gained from conversations which the writer had with some members of the Court in June of 1963. See also "Can the Court be Improved" in *European Community* (June, 1963), p. 7.

published in all four languages, but only the copy in the language actually used during the procedure before the Court is considered authentic.[1]

While it may appear from the foregoing lines that the language problem has been solved, in practice the difficulties continue and may have an adverse effect on the outcome of a specific case. This applies particularly to cases argued in the German, Italian, and Dutch language, since all of the judges and advocates-general have at least a rudimentary knowledge of French, but most of them speak and understand the other three languages only to a limited degree. As a consequence, the presentation of arguments or submission of documents in these languages is placed at a disadvantage since even the best simultaneous translation is unable to match the impression gained from listening to the presentation in the speaker's own language and written translations suffer from a similar, though less serious handicap.[2]

The Judgment

The deliberations of the Court for the formulation of the judgment are private; not even the advocates-general participate in the judicial conference. In the event that differences of opinion arise during the deliberations, a vote is taken and the opinion of the majority of the judges becomes the basis for the decision. However, the manner of voting is not indicated in the published judgment which appears as a single uniform decision.[3] Professor Donner, president of the Court, has defended this practice on the grounds that it protects the independence of the judges. Moreover, according to Professor Donner, it forces the judges to work out an agreement on the working of the decision ensuring opinions which are understandable throughout the Member States of the

---

[1] Articles 29–31 of the Rules of Procedure.

[2] Cf. also article 29(5) of the Rules of Procedure which allows the judges and advocates-general to ask questions during the oral proceedings in their own language which then are translated in the language actually used in the particular case.

[3] For details see article 27 of the Rules of Procedure. The judgment is pronounced in a public session to which the parties must be invited. See articles 63–68 for details of the judgment.

Communities and which thus contribute to the establishment of a common fund of legal notions and principles.[1]

The lack of a dissenting opinion in the judgments of the Court has been deplored. Former Judge Riese asserts that the manner of voting – whether, for instance, a case was decided by unanimous vote or by a vote of four to three – would often be of value to the parties involved in the case, particularly if one of the parties happened to be an institution of the Communities which must take into consideration the principles laid down in a judgment for its future actions and decisions.[2] Professor Zweigert believes that the institution of the dissenting opinion would add dignity to the judges of the Court and thus would enhance the authority of the judgments. He argues that it would oblige the majority of the Court to base its decisions on better and more carefully selected grounds and that it might prevent a stultification of the Court's jurisdiction because the arguments underlying the dissenting opinions compel the majority to engage in unceasing critical self-examination which eventually may lead to a gradual change in the jurisdiction of the Court.[3]

There is no question that the publication of dissenting opinions might have a salutary influence upon the jurisdiction of the Court. The jurisprudence of the U.S. Supreme Court certainly provides ample evidence that the dissenting opinions of an outstanding judge may become the jurisdiction of the future. Nevertheless, the publication of dissenting opinions of the Court of the European Communities carries with it certain dangers which outweigh its advantages. The judges of the Court are only appointed for relatively short periods and, no matter how independent they may be in theory, in practice they cannot help but look in the future and be reminded of their dependence on their national governments for re-appointment or for another position within the civil service of their countries. Thus, the institution of a dissenting opinion may well lead to an emergence of national

---

[1] Donner, *op.cit.*, p. 234.

[2] Riese, *op.cit.*, p. 273.

[3] Zweigert, *op.cit.*

interests within the Court which would not only be detrimental to the continued independence, neutrality, and impartiality of the judges, but also to the authority of the Court.[1]

Another problem in the formulation of the judgment is the language difficulty of the judges. While the Rules of Procedure, as has been seen, are quite explicit in the treatment of this problem, they do not contain any provision concerning the language to be used in the deliberations of the judges. Since the use of translators would not only prolong and encumber these deliberations, but also endanger the safeguarding of their secrecy, the practive has been to use the French language. This meant, however, that those judges whose mother tongue was not French, were more or less impeded in expressing their opinions freely, clearly, and forcefully. As a consequence, their influence upon their colleagues suffered and they were not always able to contribute to the formulation of the judgment in the same manner as if the deliberations had been conducted in their own language. Former Judge Riese relates that since all justices understood some German, he would, with their consent, at first state his position in a case in German and then would repeat his statement in French to the best of his ability.[2] Many of the judges appointed to the Court are in their late fifties or sixties and there is little doubt that new appointees must have difficulties to assimilate rapidly the intricacies and nuances of the French legal jargon.

A linguistic problem also exists in the drafting of the judgments. So far the first draft has always been worked up in the French language which later is translated into the language actually used in the procedure. This translation is then examined by the judge and his attaché whose mother tongue is the language used in the procedure. The result has frequently been that the language of the judgment has not always been fully satisfactory and that the

---

[1] If the Court in its judgment does not follow the recommendations advanced in the conclusions of the advocate-general, they may to some extent be viewed as constituting a "dissenting opinion." However, the Court takes only formal cognizance of these conclusions and does not indicate its reasons for not following them.

[2] Riese, *op.cit.*, p. 272. See also Bächle, *op.cit.*, p. 58.

style of the judgments has not been uniform.[1] Some of the judgments follow strictly the syllogistic pattern of the French courts while others are in the narrative form of the German and American Courts. The latter form might be preferable since many of the Court's decisions deal with economic matters and therefore are more lucid if the narrative style is used.

It is noteworthy that the Court has also the power of rendering judgments by default if the defendant's reply to the plaintiff's petition is either formally incorrect or submitted after the expiration of the specified time limit. In such cases the Court is required to examine not only whether it has jurisdiction, but also whether the claim of the plaintiff appears to be well founded. Judgments by default may be appealed by the defendant within one month of the receipt of the judgment.[2]

Finally, a few comments about the period of time that passes between the initiation of a case and the pronouncement of the judgment by the Court. Complaints have been voiced that this period is unduly long and these complaints do not seem to be entirely unjustified. In a few cases the proceedings have lasted as long as three and one half years; in a number of cases more than two years have passed; and in many cases a decision could only be obtained in a year and a half or more.[3] As a consequence, the actual conditions between the initiation of the suit and the pronouncement of the decision had changed so greatly in some cases that the judgment had only a theoretical meaning and was devoid of any practical significance.[4]

Review of Judgments

The power and the import of the Court is reflected by the fact that no formal appeals can be lodged against its decisions. The Court rules in the first, last, and only instance on cases before it.

---

[1] Riese, *op.cit.*, pp. 272 and 273. See also Zweigert, *op.cit.*, for other criticism regarding the form and content of the Court's judgments.

[2] Article 94 of the Rules of Procedure.

[3] For the citations of cases see Zweigert, *op.cit.*

[4] Cf. also Riese, *op.cit.*, p. 272 and Franz Breitner, "Die Bilanz des Montangerichtshofs," *Europa Archiv* (1959), pp. 515–520, at p. 520.

In this connection, the advocate-general assumes a particularly significant role since he assists in clarifying the factual and legal aspects of a case and thus performs to some degree a function which is normally fulfilled for other supreme jurisdictions by the lower courts.

Under certain, specifically prescribed circumstances, however, the Court must review a judgment previously rendered. In contrast to the rights of litigants in an American Court, parties before the Court of the European Communities have a formal right to a decision which takes into consideration the various arguments made by the contending parties. If a judgment fails to consider one of the party's principal arguments, an additional ruling on the omitted arguments may be requested. If necessary, the Court may then render a second judgment supplementing the first decision and even possibly changing it, although the latter is highly improbable.[1]

A request for a more comprehensive review may be made on the grounds that a fact has been discovered which is "capable of exerting a decisive influence" upon a judgment.[2] However, the request for review is admissible only if such a fact was unknown to the Court and to the party requesting review prior to the time the challenged decision was rendered.

Finally, the governments of Member States, the institutions of the Communities, and natural or legal persons may institute so-called third-party proceedings to contest judgments prejudicial to their rights that have been rendered without their knowledge. Petitioners for such proceedings, however, must give valid reasons why they were unable to participate in the principal proceedings before the Court and must demonstrate that they have been adversely affected in their rights by the contested decision.[3]

In two decisions rendered in 1962, the Court interpreted very narrowly the provisions regarding the contest of a judgment by

---

[1] Article 67 of the Rules of Procedure. See also Charles van Reepinghen and Paul Orianne, "La procédure devant la Cour de Justice des Communautés Européennes," *Journal des Tribunaux* (February 19, 1961), p. 126.

[2] Article 41 of the Statute of the Court.

[3] Article 39 of the Statute and article 97(1) of the Rules of Procedure.

third parties.[1] Since within the framework of the Treaties contest
of a judgment by third parties is an extraordinary legal remedy,
this narrow construction was in full accord with the accepted
rules of interpreting exceptional legal provisions. In practical
terms, however, the Court cut off the possibility of developing
these provisions into instruments for liberally filing appeals
against its judgments, a development which could have been
used as an argument to counter, at least to some degree, the
rising chorus of complaints deploring the single-instance structure
of the adjudication system within the Communities.[2]

Of course, even a more liberal interpretation of the limited
provisions for review would have made available only a modest
field expedient and would not have furnished a substitute for a
true two-tier court structure. Moreover, it would have been
extremely difficult to draw an exact dividing line as to when a
review would be permissible and when not, a factor which would
have aroused possibly even more criticism than already existed.
On the other hand, in view of the large sums of money involved
in some of the litigations before the Court and in view of the far-
reaching economic implications of some of the Court's decisions,
a one-instance Court system with very limited review possibilities
does not provide the guaranties that citizens of Western de-
mocracies normally expect to find in their systems of adjudication. While undoubtedly the advocates-general fulfill to some
degree the functions of a first instance, it should be remembered
that this function exceeds the impartial consideration of the
factual and legal aspects of a case and includes the formulation
of a judgment which might be accepted by the contending parties.
Since, as Professor Zweigert states correctly,[3] the maxim *"Le
pouvoir arrête le pouvoir"* applies also to the judicial power in
a state, efforts should be made to install, through a revision of the

[1] Société Breedband v. Société des Acieries du Temple, the High Authority, *et al.*,
Dec. Nos. 42 and 49/59, July 12, 1962, 8 Rec. 275 (1962) and the Government of the
Kingdom of Belgium v. Société Commerciale A. Vloebergh and the High Authority,
Dec. Nos. 9 and 12/62, July 12, 1962, 8 Rec. 331 (1962).
[2] See pp. 74, 75 *supra.*
[3] Zweigert, *op.cit.*

Treaties, a two-tier court system which will make available to the West European citizens the same legal guaranties and advantages on a "European" level which they justifiably expect from their national legal systems. Otherwise, a feeling of legal insecurity as far as the European level is concerned might slowly begin to permeate the Member States which would be disastrous not only for the authority and reputation of the Court, but also for the progress of European integration.

The prospects for a general revision of the Treaties are not bright at the present time, although the European Parliament, the High Authority and the EEC Commission have expressed themselves as being very much in favor of such a move.[1] But even if a revision of the Treaties became a reality, it is most doubtful that it would include the establishment of a two-tier court system since the concept of two or more instances of supra-national adjudication would be regarded most likely as too revolutionary and therefore not as yet warranted for adoption.[2] The only realistic possibility for a broader review of the Court's decision appears to lie in a revision of the Rules of Procedure which can be undertaken by the Court itself although the changes must be submitted to the Council of Ministers for unanimous approval.[3] If such a revision of the Rules of Procedure should prove to be impossible, the only remedy would be a broad interpretation of the existing provisions on the review of judgments, a practice which might turn out to be less than satisfactory.

Enforcement of Judgments

What are the powers of the Court to enforce its judgments? As has been pointed out previously,[4] in actions against the governments of the Member States only the ECSC Treaty permits

---

[1] See the speeches by Mr. Hallstein, president of the EEC Commission, Mr. Coppé, vice-president of the High Authority, and the debates during the June session of the European Parliament (Debats, Document No. 64, pp. 66–102).

[2] See also Zweigert, *op.cit.*

[3] Articles 188 EEC Treaty, 160 Euratom Treaty and 20(3), 28(5), and 44 of the Statute of the Court (ECSC). The ECSC Treaty does not require approval of the Council of Ministers except for a few provisions of the Rules of Procedure.

[4] See pp. 46, 47 *supra.*

enforcement of the Court's decisions which is effected through
the imposition of sanctions by the High Authority acting jointly
with the Council of Ministers. Against defending parties other
than the governments of the Member States, however, decisions
of the Court can be enforced in all six Member countries. This is
done by sending the judgment to the appropriate authorities of
the Member State concerned and these authorities are obligated
to execute it as if it were a local judgment. Domestic authorities
in the Member State where execution is to take place are authorized by the Treaties only to require verification of the authen-
ticity of the document containing the judgment. Once the document is verified they must grant execution in accordance with
their own rules of civil procedure.[1] National courts cannot
examine whether the Court of the Communities had jurisdiction
or whether the Community law has been correctly applied. This
procedure reflects the fact that the Court of Justice is not regarded
as a "foreign" court in the Member States.

Only the Court of the Communities itself is authorized to
suspend the execution of one of its judgments. Judgments of the
Court cannot be attacked before the national courts during the
course of the enforcement procedure. However, at least according
to the Rome Treaties, supervision as to the regularity of the
measures of execution is within the competence of the domestic
courts.[2]

---

[1] Articles 44, 92 ECSC Treaty, 187, 192 EEC Treaty, and 159, 164 Euratom
Treaty.

[2] Article 193 (4) EEC Treaty and 164 (3) Euratom Treaty. Under the ECSC Treaty
a Minister of each country is to be responsible for the execution of the Court's
judgments. See article 92 (2).

CHAPTER VI

CONCLUSIONS

In the modern history of international adjudication the Court of the European Communities is not the first regional tribunal. The leading example of an earlier regional international tribunal is the Central American Court which existed from 1908 to 1918.[1] This court was established by a convention signed in 1907 by Guatemala, Nicaragua, San Salvador, Honduras, and Costa Rica. It was composed of five judges with one judgeship allocated to each of the five participating States, and one judge and two substitute judges appointed by each of the legislatures of the States for a period of five years. The court had broad jurisdiction to deal both with disputes between the five States as well as with disputes between the States and private individuals. Although its jurisdiction was compulsory for the five States, it heard only 10 cases during the ten years of its existence and its charter was not renewed after the expiration of the period for which it was created. There were various obstacles to the court's successful operation, but the most decisive factor contributing to its demise was the refusal of Nicaragua to accept the two last decisions of the Court.[2]

In contrast to the performance of the Central American Court, the Court of the European Communities rendered during the first eleven years of its existence – specifically up to February 18, 1964 – 113 decisions and opinions and over 90 cases were pending on that date. 95 decisions and opinions grew out of the ECSC Treaty, 18 were concerned with provisions of the EEC Treaty,

[1] For other examples see Manley O. Hudson, *International Tribunals: Past and Future* (Washington, D. C., 1944), p. 172.
[2] *Ibid.*, pp. 7–8, 24, 25, 131, 172, 173.

and one decision involved a provision of the Euratom Treaty. The Court has rendered seven advisory opinions; three involved the provisions regarding the "small" revision of the ECSC Treaty, while four were issued in response to requests from national courts for interpretations of provisions of the EEC Treaty. If the number of cases decided and of those pending is taken as a criterion of successful performance and if in this respect the Court of the Communities is compared with the former Central American tribunal, the Court is obviously a success.

In the majority of litigations the complainants were private parties although proceedings were instituted in a number of cases also by the governments of the Member States and in a few instances by the organs of the Communities, i.e., the EEC Commission. In most litigations the defendants were the organs of the Community, but in several cases actions were also brought against the governments of the Member States. It is interesting to note that private enterprises and individuals have freely instituted actions against the decisions of the executive organs of the Communities and the cases pending indicate a continuance of this pattern. This phenomenon reflects the growing importance of the Court in the economic life of the European Community. It is also a clear indication that despite the recent criticism of some of its decisions [1] the Court continues to enjoy the confidence of individuals and enterprises in the Member States as being, within the realm of its competence, an acceptable arbiter of conflicting economic and social interests.

Under the ECSC Treaty the Court has liberally interpreted the provisions as to who may sue and what grounds he may assert, and thus has afforded adequate judicial protection to private parties. On the other hand, in two recent decisions involving the EEC Treaty, the Court interpreted very narrowly the provisions granting private parties the right to lodge appeals against regulations issued by the Commission and the Council of the

[1] Pp. 74–75 *supra*.

Economic Community.[1] The Court conceded that under the Rome Treaties the possibility of bringing suit against acts of the Commission and of the Council had been curtailed, but that it was not up to the Court to make a value judgment about a Treaty Provision "which was clear in its wording." This diminution of the rights of private parties to appeal against regulations affecting them has been deplored in many quarters and Advocate-General Lagrange has expressed the opinion that means must be found in the future to permit such appeals.[2]

The Court's Impact on the Formulation of Public Policy

From the discussion of the Court's jurisdictional powers [3] it is obvious that they are indeed extensive and that they exceed by far those of an international tribunal in the traditional sense. The breadth of its jurisdiction enables the Court to exercise control over most activities of the Communities and eleven years of juris-prudence reveal that the Court has been called upon to render many important decisions affecting the course of economic events, defining the powers of the Community organs and their relation-ships to the Member States, and circumscribing the rights of private individuals and enterprises which are subject to the authority of the Communities. In a number of cases, the Court was obliged to bridge gaps existing in the Treaties and to find solutions for problems not foreseen by their framers, thus per-forming a necessary and important law-creating function. If one considers that under the EEC Treaties and the Euratom Treaties the Court is authorized to control the acts of the Council of Ministers, an essentially political organ, it becomes clear that the power of the Court is not only great but that its task at times is also extremely delicate and difficult. Finally, the fact that the Court makes decisions of utmost importance as a court of the first and the last instance, significantly increases its power. The case

[1] See p. 69 *supra*, and the decision cited in footnote 5. The other decision is Fédération nationale de la boucherie *et al.* v. EEC Commission, Dec. Nos. 19–22/62 December 14, 1962, 8 Rec. 943 (1962).

[2] *European Community* (June, 1963), p. 7.

[3] See pp. 34–86 *supra*.

law developed by the Court in its decisions emerges therefore as the future law of the Communities.

In the United States the question is frequently raised as to what impact individual Supreme Court decisions have on the formulation of policy by federal and state institutions. How responsive are federal and state executive agencies, the Congress and state legislatures, and state courts to the constitutional interpretations of the Supreme Court? [1] In view of the similarity between the Court of the Communities and a federal supreme court, comparable questions come to mind with regard to the influence of the Court's decisions on the policy making of the Community institutions ("federal" institutions) and on the actions of the legislative, executive, and judicial organs of the Member States ("state" organs). A thorough analysis and evaluation of this very interesting relationship is beyond the scope of this short volume, but some cursory observations may be permitted which will suggest the Court's place in the political process of the Community.

As far as the formulation of policy by the institutions of the Communities is concerned, it has been emphasized during the discussion of the Court's jurisdictional powers that in certain instances the impact of a Court's opinion is very direct and can not be ignored nor evaded. One case in point is the "small revision" procedure under the ECSC Treaty where a negative advisory opinion on the feasibility of a proposed treaty revision must be carefully scrutinized by the High Authority and the Council of Ministers before a new acceptable proposal can be formulated.[2] Another case in point is the advisory opinion which the Court must render when a contemplated agreement between the EEC and a third country has been submitted for a ruling on the compatibility of such an agreement with the provisions of the Treaty. In the event of a negative opinion the EEC Commission

---

[1] See for instance Frank J. Sorauf, "Zorach v. Clauson: The Impact of a Supreme Court Decision," *American Political Science Review* (September, 1959), pp. 777–791, and the studies listed in footnote 2, p. 777, *ibid.*

[2] See pp. 60–63 *supra.*

must take the grounds for the Court's disapproval into account if it wants to formulate an acceptable agreement.[1] The two advisory opinions in connection with the revision of article 56 of the ECSC Treaty which would allow the High Authority to provide larger grants-in-aid for coal mines in economic difficulties, furnish ample evidence of the Court's power to influence the formulation of public policy.[2]

The Court is also in a strong position to affect policy when it annuls an act of the Community organs because the latter must take the necessary measures to implement the judgment of annulment.[3] In this connection attention should be directed to articles 174(2) EEC Treaty and 147(2) Euratom Treaty which confer upon the Court the far-reaching, but at the same time delicate power to determine "those effects of the regulation annulled which shall be deemed to remain in force."

Two hypotheses may be posited with regard to the effect of a Court's judgment upon policy formulation in the event that an act of a Community organ is annulled. First, the grounds upon which the annulment is based play an important role for the degree of influence which the Court's judgment may have on the policy formulation of the organ whose act has been annulled. If the grounds are primarily procedural as in the annulment of the EEC Commission's decision in the "German import of brandy" case,[4] the impact on policy making by the Community organ is likely to be considerably less pronounced than if the annulment is based, for instance, on an abuse of power which might have required the Court to make an extensive evaluation of the economic factors involved.[5] Second, an element bearing on the Court's influence on policy formulation is the clarity of the judgment. If the text of a judgment is somewhat ambiguous – in

---

[1] See pp. 63, 64 *supra*. For details regarding a somewhat similar advisory opinion under the Euratom Treaty see pp. 64, 65 *supra*.

[2] See pp. 61–62 *supra*.

[3] See articles 34 ECSC Treaty, 176 EEC Treaty and 149 Euratom Treaty as well as pp. 40–45 *supra*.

[4] See p. 50 *supra*.

[5] See pp. 41–42, and 66–71 *supra*.

this respect *dicta* may play an important role – the Community organ concerned (and influential economic interest groups that might stand behind it in a certain dispute) will have greater latitude in the interpretation of such a judgment and therefore the influence of the Court on policy making by this organ will be correspondingly reduced. An interesting example of the effects of an annulment judgment not only on the Community organ whose decision has been annuled, but also on the policy formulation of a Member State is found in the case of the Dutch Coal Mining Association of Limburg v. the High Authority which has been discussed earlier.[1] The Court annulled the decision of the High Authority in which the latter refused to take action against subsidy payments made by the West German government to German coal miners. As the result of this judgment the Federal government began to take steps to alter its policy with regard to these subsidies.

The Court's impact on policy formulation makes itself also felt when a judgment of the Court declares that a Community organ has failed to take a required action. Although the judgment of the Court proclaims only that the inaction of the Community organ is illegal and does not prescribe the detailed action to be taken, in practice the rationale of the judgment is bound to have a weighty influence on the policy underlying the action which the Community organ concerned must take.[2]

Even if the Court sustains the contentions of the Community organs in certain cases, it may play a role in policy formulation because it thereby confirms the specific policy of an organ embodied in a regulation or decision and thus strengthens the hand of this organ to pursue this line of policy. Of course, an organ may want to change its policy even if it has found approval by the Court. An example of such change is the decision of the High Authority early in 1963 to permit the Ruhr coal producers to sell their products through two sales agencies instead of three. Previously the High Authority had considered three agencies as

[1] See p. 53 *supra*.
[2] See pp. 41, and 70–71 *supra*.

the minimum requirement consistent with the anti-trust provisions of the ECSC Treaty and this policy had been upheld by the Court in its judgment of May 18, 1962. However, the Court will have the last word in this matter because the Dutch government has filed a complaint with the Court alleging that the High Authority's latest decision was legally defective.[1]

The fine hand of the Court seems also to be detectable in the formulation of policy underlying the very important Regulation No. 17 spelling out the details of the EEC anti-trust law. While it is difficult to determine the exact role of the Court in the drafting of this regulation, some measure of co-operation with the policy-making group in the EEC Commission can be inferred from the text of the Bosch judgment rendered in 1962.[2]

The impact of the Court's decisions on the development of policy in the Member States has been illustrated on several occasions during the discussion of the jurisdictional powers of the Court. Italian, Belgian, and Luxembourg Treaty violations impeding the functioning of the Common Market were declared illegal by the Court and resulted in changes of policy by the governments of these countries. The dispute regarding the German freight rates for coal came to a happy conclusion when German government adjusted its rate structure in compliance with the decisions of the Court. As a consequence of the Court's judgment in the Humblet case the Belgian government altered its policy and ceased to take into consideration a Community civil servant's salary when computing the rate of his or her spouse's income tax.[3] The policy adjustments in preparation by the German government with respect to the subsidy payments for German miners have been noted above.

In the struggle over the application of the ECSC anti-trust provisions to the Ruhr coal sales organization, the German government has strongly sided with the stand taken by the coal

[1] See pp. 77–80 *supra*.
[2] For details see *supra*, pp. 56–58. It would not be surprising if the Court had not been asked by Community organs on other occasions to assist in the drafting of important regulations by informally presenting its expert opinion.
[3] Cf. pp. 51–52.

producers and considerations of economic and social policy with respect to this issue have deeply involved the Federal government. The case initiated by the Dutch government against the High Authority, the primary aim of which undoubtedly was to ensure the proper application of the ECSC Treaty by the High Authority but which possibly also was intended to test the fortitude of the Court, will give the justices another opportunity to review this difficult problem. Since, as has been pointed out earlier[1], this is a problem which requires for its solution political rather than judicial action because it is so deeply entangled with the drastic economic changes which during the last few years have affected the coal industry, the wisdom of the Court will be supremely taxed. There is little question, however, that a judgment completely committed to the maintenance of the 1962 *status quo* (three sales agencies as approved by the May 18, 1962 decision) will not induce the German government to adjust its policies accordingly. On the other hand, such a judgment may become the trigger for the badly needed revision of the Treaty's anti-trust provisions in order to adapt them to the economic reality as it exists today.

Finally, a few comments are in order about the influence of the Court upon proceedings involving Community law before the national tribunals in the Member States, which may be compared to "state" courts in a federal system. From the discussion of the Treaty provisions concerning the uniform interpretation of the Treaties and of the acts of the Community institutions [2] it has become apparent that the effectiveness of the Court in maintaining uniformity in interpretation by the national courts is limited. One weakness lies in the ECSC Treaty whose provisions in this respect contain several gaps. Another, and possibly more serious weakness, is the inability of the Court to compel national courts to refer to it any problematical questions regarding the interpretation of the Treaties or Community acts even if such a question has been raised by one of the parties in litigation before a national court. The fact that a number of national tribunals has

[1] Pp. 77–80 *supra.*
[2] Pp. 54–60 *supra.*

failed to forward to the Court of the Communities questions of interpretation for which a requirement for referral obviously existed demonstrates the seriousness of the deficiency in the Court's powers, a deficiency which in the long run may have grave consequences for the development of a uniform Community law.

Despite this particular deficiency in its powers, the Court's overall influence – actual and potential, direct and indirect – upon policy formulation within the framework of the Communities must be regarded as remarkably extensive. It is not surprising therefore, that voices have been heard which talk of the prospect of a "government by judges." [1] Expressing a somewhat similar view, the Tenth Report of the "Committee of the Presidents" of the European Parliament, dated June 25, 1962, complained that the Court exercised a degree of influence upon the High Authority which was much greater than that normally possessed by a supreme court upon an executive organ.[2] While it is correct that because of the High Authority's timid exercise of its power during the last few years the Court occasionally has been thrust into a position where it had to assume leadership,[3] fears of a "government by judges" appear to be completely unwarranted. In fact, as has been seen earlier,[4] the Court has always taken great pains to maintain the basic distribution of powers that the Treaties have provided for the relations between the organs of the Communities. In addition, it has always delimited with meticulous care the allocation of competences between the Communities and the Member States making sure that no organ of the Communities, including the Court, would encroach upon the powers "reserved to the States." [5]

---

[1] For instance Bye, *op.cit.*, p. 267.
[2] Paragraphs 93 and 99.
[3] Lagrange, "The Role of the Court," pp. 416 and 417.
[4] Pp. 40–45 *supra*.
[5] See pp. 52, 54 *supra*.

Conclusions

The Court's Contribution to Political Integration

The extensive jurisdictional powers of the Court of the European Communities bring to mind the question whether this institution can contribute in any manner to the political integration of the Member States. The contributions to the strength of the Federal government in the United States which were made in the last century by several important Supreme Court decisions under the leadership of Chief Justice John Marshall are well known.[1] Is it likely that the Court of the European Communities can play a similar role? Are there other ways by which the Court can aid in the attainment of West European unity?

Before these questions can be answered even tentatively, another equally difficult question must be examined, namely whether or not the judges are predisposed toward the concept of European unity. While the basic task of the justices is the observance of law in the application of the Treaties, any interpretation of the provisions of the Treaties opens up the possibility of choice from among a number of legally acceptable principles and techniques. In such choices, the political philosophies of the justices might be consciously or unconsciously reflected. Therefore, if the judges were generally adverse to the concept of a politically united Europe, the likelihood is remote that choices to be made by them in rendering decisions would favor political integration.

It is of course very difficult to gauge a judge's political philosophy and to determine his predisposition toward a certain concept. Such an undertaking has to be based mainly on circumstantial evidence and the inferences drawn from this evidence may not be entirely valid. Nevertheless, an attempt will be made to use certain published facts and statements as a basis for an estimate of the values and views held by the present judges of the Court.

Since the average age of the judges of the Court is almost 61 years, most of them have had first-hand experience with the

---

[1] One of the most forceful decisions in this respect was McCulloch v. Maryland, 4 Wheaton 316 (1819).

miseries of two world wars.[1] One may assume with some justification, therefore, that the judges may see in a united Europe a possible means of precluding the use of war for the settlement of disputes between the European states. In addition, some of the judges participated prominently in international conferences, held positions with international organizations, and were active in movements for a united Europe [2] which suggests an identification of these individuals with the fundamental goal of international organization, the establishment of an order transcending the jurisdiction of the nation-state. Publications by the judges as well as papers presented at professional gatherings also reflect attitudes favoring the political integration of Western Europe.[3]

Finally, an additional insight into the values held by the members of the Court can be gained by a perusal of the speeches made during the ceremonies which took place when either a new judge was sworn in or when a judge was given a farewell reception. In most of President Donner's speeches on such occasions one can discover expressions of his commitment to the idea of European unity. In his address welcoming Dr. Strauss to the Court, which was delivered in February 1963, shortly after the De Gaulle debacle, Professor Donner stated that "since the political impetus [for European integration] will possibly slacken for some time to come, it is incumbent upon the organs [of the Communities] to be all the more conscious of their role as the institutionalized carriers of the European idea." [4] In several of his speeches Pro-

---

[1] The youngest judge is Professor Donner, the president of the Court; he was born in 1918.

[2] For details see *Annuaire-Manuel du Parlement Européen*, (1961–62), pp. 109–112.

[3] For instance, Delvaux, *op.cit.*, p. 11; A. M. Donner, "La justice, facteur d'unité et d'égalité du droit," *Journal des Tribunaux*, November 25, 1962, pp. 649–651; Walter Strauss, *Fragen der Rechtsangleichung im Rahmen der Europäischen Gemeinschaften* (Frankfurt/Main, 1959), pp. 38, 39; Robert Lecourt, The Development of European Law," *European Community* (June, 1963), p. 10, and "L'Europe dans le prétoire," *Le Monde*, February 23, 1963; and Alberto Trabucchi, *Un nouveau droit*, paper presented April 6, 1963, at the Center for the Documentation and Study of the European Communities at the University of Ferrara (Italy).

[4] Address of February 6, 1963 (Mimeographed copy). See also the addresses of Professor Donner on the occasions when Mr. Lecourt and Mr. Trabucchi took their oaths of office (Mimeographed copies.)

fessor Donner emphasized the constitutional role of the Court, possibly a reflection of his hope to see the Court develop eventually into the supreme court of a European federation. The responses given by the departing judges to the speeches of Professor Donner also contain favorable references to the concept of European unity. Mr. Catalano stressed that what is important is the creation of a European jurisprudence, inspired by a European spirit and animated by a European conscience which must be at the bottom of all of our actions for the sake of our future and the future of our children.[1] Others expressed their satisfaction that they were able to participate in the establishment of the European Community.[2]

In view of the evidence presented the assumption seems to be justified that at least a majority of the judges looks with favor upon the political integration of the Member States. However, up to now, this attitude has not generally resulted in a strong jurisprudence of the Court in terms of political integration. An exception is the ruling rendered by the Court early in 1963 in the case of Van Gend & Loos. In this ruling the Court held that the Common Market Treaty established certain private rights for individuals within the Member States that must be honored and enforced by the national courts even against their own governments. Overruling strong objections of the Dutch, Belgian, and German governments, the Court's opinion strengthened the prospects for political unification by boldly asserting that certain provisions of the Treaties did not only create obligations on the part of the Member governments but constituted norms that were on the same level as rules promulgated by the national legislatures.[3]

While so far the Van Gend ruling is the only decision of the Court with a strong integrative effect and while most of its other decisions appear to be completely unaffected by whatever attitude the judges may hold with regard to European unification, some

[1] March 8, 1962 (Mimeographed copy).
[2] See responses of Mr. Riese on February 6, 1963 and of Mr. Rueff on May 18, 1962 (Mimeographed copies).
[3] See pp. 58, 59 *supra*. This decision was confirmed by the ruling in the Da Costa en Schaake case.

judgments have tended to advance the fortunes of political integration very subtly in an indirect manner. These are the judgments in which the Court has sustained the Commission in its complaints of Treaty violations by Member States [1] and those in which it has rejected appeals of Member governments against decisions of the High Authority or of the Commission.[2] It is significant that none of the governments of the Member States has defied the adverse judgments of the Court but that they have complied with them. This compliance has strengthened the supranational authority of the Court and has increased the respect for the supranational organs of the Communities. These minor gains in the struggle for European unity might not have been made or, if made, might have been lost again if the Court had pursued a course in its jurisprudence pressuring aggressively for political integration. The reason is that such a course might well have aroused vigorous resentment within the governments of the Member States and among politically influential economic groups with the result that the prospects for political integration might actually have been damaged. That the Court refrained from such a course, is a testimony to its political wisdom.

While then in terms of political integration one can not detect a generally strong note in the jurisprudence of the Court, its decisions have stressed again and again the goals of economic integration as the fundamental principles of the ECSC and EEC Treaties. Although the judgments of the Court have reflected a desire to render primarily decisions which are practicable within the framework of the Treaties and which take into consideration the sometimes painful economic changes and dislocations brought about by the goals set forth in the Treaties, the Court has never overlooked the objective of economic integration if this was pertinent for the case it was deciding. In fact, the Court has made every effort to guide the governments of the Member States, the organs of the Communities, and private enterprises toward the

[1] See pp. 45, 47 *supra*.

[2] See pp. 48–50 *supra*. So far the Court has ruled on 12 appeals by Member governments against decisions of the High Authority and the EEC Commission; in several cases the contentions of the Member governments have been upheld.

full implementation of this objective with a gentle and under-standing, yet albeit firm hand.

The decisions rendered by the Court in support of economic integration in the Member States and the mere fact that the Court is in existence and functioning may also have implications for the furtherance of political integration. In an interesting and thought-provoking article appearing in 1962, Professor Donner pointed out that in the evolution of the modern Western states political unity was realized first in those countries where a central authority was in a position to impose its own administration of justice and to maintain it in the face of centrifugal feudal and regional forces.[1] Regular and uniform administration of justice thus became a strong element of political integration in France and Britain, whereas the absence of such an administration of justice in the Holy Roman Empire was one of the causes leading to its dissolution. Professor Donner also stressed that unity and uniformity of the administration of justice produced in the long run uniformity of substantive law because the differences of regional laws began to be resented as unnecessary shackles and later became to be viewed as unjust and arbitrary. In turn, the uniformity of law and jurisprudence tended to pave the way for economic integration and development. The rapid expansion of industry and commerce in Britain and France during the 18th and 19th centuries would hardly have been possible without the creation of a uniform legal base. In turn, these economic and legal developments contributed toward greater national unity.

While, in contrast to the historical examples to which Professor Donner alluded, no central authority of political significance exists at present within the West European Community, regular and uniform administration of justice prevails on the "European" level. There is also in operation a significant interplay between the administration of justice provided by the Court and economic integration which bears some similarity to the relationship be-tween the dispensation of justice and industrial expansion de-scribed in the preceding paragraph. The impetus in this interplay

[1] Donner, "La justice,...." p. 649.

is furnished by the institutionalized process of economic integration, because the progressive fusion of the economies of the six Member States as envisaged by the Treaties requires a stable legal roadmap. Economic interests anticipating to benefit from an integrated economy[1] and eager to realize the goal of a common market in Western Europe have been demanding uniformity of those national laws which are crucial for the accomplishment of economic unity. Foreseeing this development, the EEC Treaty recommends to the Member States "the approximation of their respective municipal laws to the extent necessary for the functioning of the Common Market."[2] Conferences aimed at harmonizing the national laws in the field of banking, patents, and the establishment of subsidiaries and branches have been held or are scheduled in the near future. Yet, even if agreement is reached between the conferees, it takes considerable time to pass the appropriate parallel legislation in the six Member States. In the meantime, if economic integration is to proceed at a dynamic pace, the economic interests within the Member States must look to the Court for remedies and uniform legal guidelines whenever the realization of the Common Market is threatened by *lacunae* and ambiguities in the provisions of the Treaties.

Of course, so far the majority of the Court's decisions has been rendered in response to complaints from those whose interests have been harmed by the process of economic integration. In some of these cases the Court was called upon to arbiter serious conflicts of important economic interests with social and political implications. Yet the case law developed from these decisions has also been a necessary part of the legal road map required to guide the economic enterprises of the Member States toward the attainment of the goals set by the Treaties. As economic inte-

[1] Some of the smaller industrial enterprises, especially in France, have not as yet benefitted from the Common Market but many mergers have taken place to make these small units more competitive. See also Michael Shanks and John Lambert, *The Common Market, Today- and Tomorrow* (New York, 1962), pp. 136–9 and Frank, *op. cit.*, pp. 147–150.

[2] Article 3h; see also articles 100–102 of the EEC Treaty which authorizes direct intervention by institutions of the EEC to reconcile the legislative and administrative rules of Member States under certain specified conditions.

gration progresses toward the goal of economic unity, the case law of the Court will therefore evolve as an increasingly vital ingredient of the legal structure upon which the integrated economy in the Member States will rest. In this process it may well become the forerunner of a single body of European law and may constitute a strong, unifying force for the eventual creation of a federated Western Europe.

The sequence of events in contemporary Europe thus seems to be different from the historical model cited by Professor Donner. There, uniform administration of justice imposed by a central political authority triggered the development of uniform substantive law which, in turn, provided the basis for greater economic development. In today's Western Europe no central political authority exists but the demands of economics integration institutionalized by the three Treaties are obliging a uniform administration of justice, operating exclusively on the "European" level, to create the beginnings of a body of substantive, and possibly procedural, European case law based on the provisions of the Treaties. As this body of European law is supplemented by parallel legislation in the Member States and as it is increasingly applied by the judges of the national courts in the Member States,[1] thereby making the people in these countries more and more conscious of the existence of a European law, it will provide increasingly strong leverage for the establishment of a central political authority. The Court, therefore, by its mere existence and functioning, is in a position to make a contribution to the political integration of the Member States although the degree of its effectiveness will depend on political and economic factors and forces beyond the influence of the Court. However, one can hypothesize that the more decisions the Court renders, the greater will be the potential of its contribution.

[1] See for instance the judgment of the Court of Appeals, Paris (France), of January 26, 1963 and the comments by Jean Robert in *Common Market Law Review* (September 1963), pp. 218–231. See also the examples cited by Mr. Trabucchi in his paper given at the University of Ferrara (cf. the citation on p. 116, footnote 3 *supra*), namely, the judgments of the Administrative Court in Berlin of October 26, 1962, and of the Italian *Conseil d'Etat* of November 7, 1962.

Conclusions

The future of the Court itself is closely tied to the progress of economic and political integration in the Member States. With the progression of economic integration the workload of the Court is likely to increase and the heavier workload may make it necessary to expand the number of judges in the future. The Treaties have anticipated this possibility; upon the request of the Court, the Council of Ministers may by unanimous vote increase the number of judges.[1] If progress were made toward political integration, the prestige of the Court and of the judges would be greatly enhanced since in the distance would loom the possibility of a multi-tier court system similar to that of the federal courts in the United States.[2] Such a prospect would tend to strengthen the favorable pre-disposition of the justices toward the concept of European unity and thus might exert a subtle influence upon the future jurisprudence of the Court.

Unquestionably, the challenges with which a supranational court is confronted are great. The determination of what is law is much more complicated for a supranational court than for a national court. *Lacunae* in the application of the Treaties are much more frequent than they are in the national law. Differences in the legal training and in the basic intellectual concepts of the individual judges add to the difficulties. Yet the Court of Justice of the European Communities has in general measured up to these challenges and has successfully established a new dimension in international adjudication. Jean Monnet's prediction made more than ten years ago that the Court would eventually become a European Federal Supreme Court may come true in future years. Moreover, it is not inconceivable that the Court may serve as a model for the creation of similar tribunals in the future such as an Atlantic Community High Court [3] or the projected Arab Court of Justice.[4]

---

[1] Articles 32 ECSC Treaty, 165 EEC Treaty, and 137 Euratom Treaty.

[2] In this respect cf. also the publications of judges Trabucchi, Lecourt, and Strauss listed on p. 116, footnote 3 *supra*.

[3] Suggested in the *Report of the United States Citizens Commission on NATO*, House Document No. 433, 97th Congress, 2nd Session (Washington, 1962), pp. 11–12.

[4] See E. Foda, *The Projected Arab Court of Justice* (The Hague, 1957).

SELECTED BIBLIOGRAPHY

BOOKS

Bächle, Hans-Ulrich, *Die Rechtstellung der Richter am Gerichtshof der Europäischen Gemeinschaften*. Berlin, 1961

Bebr, Gerhard, *Judicial Control of the European Communities*. New York, 1962.

Delvaux, Louis, *La Cour de Justice de la Communauté Européenne du Charbon et de l'Acier*. Gembloux, France, 1956.

Haas, Ernest B., *The Uniting of Europe*. Stanford, California, 1958.

Hallstein, Walter, *United Europe, Challenge and Opportunity*. Cambridge, Massachusettes, 1962.

Hudson, Manley O., *International Tribunals: Past and Future*. Washington, D.C., 1944.

Lister, Louis, *Europe's Coal and Steel Community*. New York, 1960.

Mason, Henry L., *The European Coal and Steel Community, Experiment in Supranationalism*. The Hague, 1955.

Mathijsen, Pierre, *Le droit de la Communauté Européenne du Charbon et de l'Acier, Une étude des sources*. The Hague, 1958.

Reuter, Paul, *La Communauté Européenne du Charbon et de l'Acier*. Paris, 1953.

Rosenne, Shabtai, *The International Court of Justice*. Leyden, 1961.

Schwartz, Bernard, *French Administrative Law and the Common Law World*. New York, 1954.

Stein, E. and Nicholson, T. L. (eds.), *American Enterprise in the European Common Market A Legal Profile*, Ann Arbor, Michigan, 1960.

Stein, E., "The New Institutions".

Stein, E. and Hay, Peter, ''New Legal Remedies: A Survey.''

Strauss, Walter, *Fragen der Rechtsangleichung im Rahmen der Europäischen Gemeinschaften*. Frankfurt/Main, 1959.

Valentine, D. G., *The Court of Justice of the European Coal and Steel Community*, The Hague, 1955.

Wohlfarth, E., Everling, U., Glässner, H. J., Sprung, R., *Die Europäische Wirtschaftsgemeinschaft, Kommentar zum Vertrag*. Berlin and Frankfurt a.M., 1960.

Selected Bibliography

PERIODICALS

Carstens, Karl, "Die kleine Revision des Vertrages über die Europäische Gemeinschaft fur Kohle und Stahl," *Zeitschrift fur ausländisches Recht und Völkerrecht*, (January 1961), 1–37.

Daig, Hans-Wolfram, "Die Gerichtsbarkeit der Europäischen Wirtschaftsgemeinschaft und der Europäischen Atomgemeinschaft," *Archiv des Öffentlichen Rechts*, (1958), 132–208.

—, "Die vier ersten Urteile des Gerichtshofes der Europäischen Gemeinschaft für Kohle und Stahl," *Juristenzeitung* (1955), 361–373.

Donner, A. M., "La justice, facteur d'unité et d'égalité du droit," *Journal des Tribunaux*, (November 25, 1962), 649–651.

—, "The oCurt of Justice of the European Communities," *The Record of the Bar of New York*, (May 1962), 232–243.

Feld, Werner, "The Civil Service of the European Communities: Legal and Political Aspects," *Journal of Public Law*, (Vol. 12, 1963), 68–85.

—, "The Judges of the Court of Justice of the European Communities," *Villanova Law Review*, (Fall 1963), 37–58.

Hay, Peter, "Federal Jurisdiction of the Common Market Court," *American Journal of Comparative Law*, (1963), 21–40.

Houtte, M. A. van, "La Cour de Justice de la Communauté Européenne du Charbon et de l'Acier," *European Yearbook*, (Vol. II), 183–222.

Lagrange, Maurice, "La Cour de Justice de la CECA," *Revue du Droit Public et de la Science Politique*, (1954), 417–435.

—, "Les Pouvoirs de la Haute Authorité et l'application du Traité de Paris," *Revue du Droit Public et de la Science Politique*, (January–February 1961), 40–58.

—, "The Role of the Court of Justice of the European Communities as Seen Through its Case Law," *Law and Contemporary Problems*, (Summer, 1961), 400–417.

Lecourt, Robert, "The Development of European Law," *European Community*, (June 1963), 10.

—, "L'Europe dans le prétoire," *Le Monde*, (February 23, 1963).

McMahon, J. F., "The Court of the European Communities: Judicial Interpretation and International Organization," *The British Yearbook of International Law*, (1961), 320–350.

Mattern, K. H., "Rechtsgrundlage and Praxis der Montanversammlung," *Neue Juristische Wochenschrift*, (1954), 218–219.

Reepinghen, Charles van and Orianne, Paul, "La procédure devant la Cour de Justice des Communautés Européennes," *Journal des Tribunaux*, (February 19, 1961), 126.

Reuter, Paul, "Juridical and Institutional Aspects of European Regional Communities," *Law and Contemporary Problems*, (Summer 1961), 381–399.

Riese, Otto, "Erfahrungen aus der Praxis des Gerichtshofes der Europäischen Gemeinschaft für Kohle und Stahl," *Deutsche Richterzeitung,* (1958), 270–274.

Seeler, Hans-Joachim, "Politische Intergration and Gewaltenteilung," *Europa-Archiv,* (1960), 13–24.

Stone, Victor J., "The Court and Anglo-Saxon Law," *European Community,* (June 1963), 8–9.

Thermaat, P. Verloren van, "Gedanken zur Wettbewerbspolitik im Gemeinsamen Markt," *Wirtschaft und Wettbewerb,* (July/August 1963), 555–564.

Zellentin, Gerda, "The Economic and Social Committee," *Journal of Common Market Studies,* (1962), 22–28.

INDEX

Access to Court, 34
Acts of Community Organs, 54, 55, 66
Advisory Opinions, 62, 63, 65, 110
Advocate-General, 17, 21–27, 29, 32, 64, 95, 96, 98, 100, 102, 103
Annulment, 68, 110, 111
Anti-Trust Provisions, 56–58, 62, 76, 78, 79, 112, 113
Attachés of the Court, 26

Bebr, Professor G., 89
Belgium, 1, 5, 16, 17, 47, 59, 76, 117

Catalano, Nicola, 16, 19, 29, 30, 117
Civil Jurisdiction, 80
Common Consent, 14, 17
Coudenhove-Kalergi, Count, 1
Council of Ministers, 6–12, 16, 23, 34, 40, 41, 43, 62–64, 66, 71, 79, 86, 88, 104, 105, 108, 109, 122

Decisions, 54, 55, 69
de Gaulle, 11, 60, 116
Delvaux, M. Louis, 2, 16, 28–30
Détournement de Pouvoir, 67, 68, 89
Directives, 54, 55
Discretionary Powers, 89
Donner, A. M., 16, 17, 29, 35, 74, 98, 116, 117, 119, 121

Economic Evaluation, 103, 110, 118
Economic and Social Committee, 10
Enterprise, 73, 108
European Investment Bank, 34, 35, 85
E.E.C. Commission, 6–12, 15, 17, 22, 29, 35, 37, 47–50, 57, 65, 82
Euratom Commission, 6–10, 12, 15, 17, 20, 22
European Parliament, 5, 9–13, 16, 21, 61, 79, 104

France, 1, 5, 16, 17, 21, 31, 32, 119, 120

French *Counseil d'Etat*, 22, 32, 40, 88
Full Review, 81, 82, 85

Germany, 16, 17, 21, 31, 49, 59, 77, 117

Hammes, Ch. Leon, 16, 20, 28–30
High Authority, 6–9, 11, 12, 16, 17, 34, 40–42, 44–46, 48–51, 53, 55, 60–63, 65, 69, 70, 72, 73, 75–82, 85, 86, 88, 93, 104, 105, 109, 111–114, 118
Hirsch, Etienne, 20
Hoesch Co., 73
Houtte, Albert van, 33

"Implied Powers", 43
Inaction, Appeal Against, Right to Bring, 41, 70, 71
International Court of Justice, Statute of, 16, 18, 21, 24, 38, 44
Interpretation of Treaties, 91, 93, 113
Italy, 1, 5, 11, 16, 17, 45, 49

Kleffens, Adrianus van, 16, 20, 29, 30
Kloeckner Co., 73

Lagrange, Maurice, 21, 28, 32, 39, 48, 56, 68, 89, 90, 92, 93, 97, 108
Lecourt, Robert, 16, 28–30, 122
Luxembourg, 1, 2, 5, 16, 17, 24, 47

Mannesmann Co., 73–75
Municipal Law, 88, 89, 92

National Courts, 93, 105, 113
Netherlands, 1, 5, 11, 16, 17, 56, 59, 79, 117

Objectives of Treaties, 93
"Official Fault", 83, 84

Penalty Payments, 86
"Personal Fault", 83, 84

126

Index

Petrick, Johannes, 78
Pilotti, Massimo, 16, 17, 20, 29, 30
Poincaré, R., 30
Precedent, 74
Preliminary Decision, 55–60
Preliminary Investigation, 94, 95
Private Parties, 66, 70, 94, 95, 107, 108

Quasi-Legislative Powers, 7–9, 11, 39, 54, 66

Recommendations, 54, 55, 69
Registrar of the Court, 25, 26, 29, 33
Regulations, 54, 55, 57, 69
"Reserved Powers", 53, 114
Riese, Otto, 16–18, 20, 29, 30, 96, 99, 100
Roemer, Joseph, 21, 28, 33, 45, 92
Rossi, Rino, 16, 28–30
Rueff, Jacques, 16, 29, 30, 117
Ruhr, 76–79, 111
Rules of Procedure, 25, 26, 28, 94–98, 100–102, 104

Schmidhauser, John R., 31
Schuman, Robert, 2
Scrap Iron, 72, 73, 75
Serrarens, Joseph, 16, 20, 29, 30
Simon, Gabriel, 35, 82, 92
"Small Revision", 79, 88, 107, 109
Stammberger, Minister, 19
Starke, Minister, 18
Stay of Execution, 105
Strauss, Walter, 16, 18, 19, 28–31, 116, 122
Supranational Powers, 1–3

Trabucchi, Alberto, 16, 19, 28, 29, 122
Treaty Violation, 83, 118

Ultra Vires, 67
United States, 31, 75, 109

Zweigert, Professor Konrad, 97, 99, 103